DANCE AUDITIONS

★★★★★★★★★★★★★★★★★★★★★★★★★★★★★★★★★★★★

DANCE AUDITIONS

★★★★★★★★★★★★★★★★★★★★★★★★★★★★★★★★★★★★★

Preparation, Presentation, Career Planning

ERIC BRANDT NIELSEN

University of Florida

**With Professional Insights From
Ballet, Broadway, Las Vegas, Modern, and TV**

by
Wayne Cilento★ Daniel Duell★ Richard Englund★ Laura
Glenn★ Barbara Hanks★ Erick Hawkins★ Geoffrey Holder★
Robert Joffrey★ Phyllis Lamhut★ Adrian Le Peltier★ Henry Le
Tang★ Murray Louis★ Donald Mahler★ Tommy Peel★ Patricia
Rozow★ Denny Shearer★ Tony Stevens★ Lee Theodore★
Tommy Tune★ Dan Wagoner★ Charles Ward★ Dennis Wayne★
Rebecca Wright★

PRINCETON BOOK COMPANY,
PUBLISHERS
PRINCETON, NEW JERSEY

To
Marjorie June Cone Nielsen
and
Ove Brandt Nielsen
for their
dedication to my
life's commitment
in dance

Library of Congress Catalog Card Number 83-063189
ISBN 916622-33-9 hardbound edition
ISBN 916622-31-2 paperbound edition

Printed in the United States of America

Design by Ann Schlesinger
Typeset by Delmas

ACKNOWLEDGMENTS
★★★

The author wishes to thank all the professional artists who contributed to make this book possible.

Special thanks are also due to Charles Woodford, who saw the value in my book; Marnee Hollis, my assistant, who helped me through the rough times; a great group of University of Florida students, who posed for many of the photographs; and to Chris Stark, David Heath, and Gweneth West for their invaluable help.

Especially to be commended are the photographers: Michael Avedon, Randy Batista, Otto M. Berk, Roy Blakey, Tom Caravaglia, Stephen Driscoll, J. Elbers, Arthur Elgort, Paul Hustoles, Douglas Mackenzie, Herbert Migdoll, Jack Mitchell, and Hans Pelgrum.

PREFACE

★★★★★★★★★★★★★★★★★★★★★★★★★★★★★★★★★★

The lack of informative material on dance auditioning approaches and methods has been evident to me, both while teaching on the college level and performing as a professional dancer. I have noticed repeatedly that well-trained dancers, especially on the college level, are unaware of the preparations that are necessary to present themselves properly to a prospective employer.

A professional dancer should know how to organize a resume and portfolio as well as understand the steps in making a favorable impression when auditioning. It is ludicrous to think that dancers, who train and prepare themselves for years, are many times deficient in one vital skill—job application. There is an abundance of well-written books available for actors, but not one comprehensive text that gives dancers an insight into the auditioning process.

The prime objective of this book is to provide an informative and practical handbook for dancers. It is unique in that it combines the knowledge and advice of professionals with an understanding of the educational needs of students who want to become professional dancers. The dancers and choreographers who were interviewed for this book have had many years of experience on Broadway and television, and in ballet, modern, film, and Las Vegas-style show dancing. These interviews give the reader first-hand insight into the requirements, problems, and discoveries in auditioning for a specific dance job.

CONTENTS

★★★★★★★★★★★★★★★★★★★★★★★★★★★★★★★★★★★

1

FIRST IMPRESSIONS
★★★★★★★★★★★★★★★★★★★★★★★★★★★★★★★★★★★★

When auditioning for any job, always remember that first impressions are very important. An audition often begins the minute you hand your resume to the auditioner. The way you look and handle yourself through the entire process of an audition can be just as important as performing the dance combinations well.

APPEARANCE

To look your best, you must know how to use makeup properly, groom your hair so that it does not get in your face while dancing, and wear the proper dance attire.

Makeup

Makeup requires evaluation for each audition. For example, the makeup worn for a modern dance audition need not be as elaborate as that worn for a show dancing audition. It is inappropriate for men to wear any makeup; neatness is more important.

Since facial attractiveness is extremely important in *show dancing,* women should use evening makeup with special attention given to the eyes. Show auditionees usually perform on large stages, so that the overall effect of makeup must look good

1

from a distance. A pair of eyelashes will also help to project and enhance the eye makeup.

When preparing for *Broadway, television,* or *ballet* auditions, women should use light makeup to highlight their facial features. Apply little or no makeup for *modern dance* auditions, since the natural look is more important.

Above all, care should be taken to avoid an "overdone" look that may differ from your resume photograph. An auditioner often depends on your photograph for final evaluations following the audition as well as for making decisions on callbacks. If he has seen sixty or more dancers during an audition, the photograph, rather than the name on the resume, becomes vital in recalling the auditionee's face. If you have used excessive makeup or have changed the style of your hair after obtaining your resume photograph, it may not only confuse the auditioner but accidently cause him to disregard your resume when sorting out his final list of dancers.

Hair

Your hair should always be out of your face during an audition. Women can usually pin their hair, while men should consider using hairspray if they find that their hair does not stay in place. Be aware of your particular problems and secure the hair well. You want to look your best during as well as after the dance combinations. Most *ballet* auditioners will expect women to conform to a traditional hair code, which usually consists of pulling the hair completely back and away from the face and securing it tightly in a bun at the back of the head. Stories that dancers are fined in professional ballet companies for not spraying down hair wisps should be taken seriously, so get in the habit of taking care of your hair properly.

Dance Attire

Shoes. Ballet slippers and pointe shoes may be standard equipment, but all dancers should also have character shoes in their wardrobe. Part of a *ballet* audition may include character dance, so women should have a pair of black character shoes with a one- or two-inch heel. Even if you are not asked to perform character dance at the audition, most ballet companies require their dancers to have their own character shoes because character dances, such as czardas, mazurkas, and even Spanish heel work, are almost always performed in full-length classical ballets. Women also use character shoes for jazz, although occasionally they perform in jazz oxfords and often prefer them for jazz class.

Male dancers will find the need to invest in character shoes and jazz oxfords for several good reasons. If the male dancer is doing character dance, he needs a good leather-soled shoe with a solid heel, which the jazz oxford, with its rubber sole and heel, does not provide. The character shoe is also a recommended dress shoe for musical comedy work and a standard shoe used for applying taps. Many dancers try to convert their only pair of character shoes into tap shoes when the need arises. Unfortunately, the constant removal of taps and rubber supports is a tiresome process and eventually damages the shoes. It is a good idea to have two pairs of character shoes and use one pair exclusively for taps. On the other hand, doing jazz in character shoes is often difficult and cumbersome because they are not as pliable as jazz oxfords and lack the rubber sole and heel which help tremendously to prevent slipping. It is certainly worthwhile to have both.

In auditions for *Broadway, television,* or a *show,* men perform primarily in jazz oxfords and women in character shoes. In most shows, women dance in character shoes because of the flattering line and added height. Certain shows also have tap dancing, so stuff a pair of tap shoes in your dance bag before leaving for the audition.

You will find that dancers are asked to change shoes more frequently than other dancewear, so make sure footwear is on your priority list for audition preparations. As a professional dancer you should have the following shoes in your wardrobe:

Joni Burton putting on tap shoes. Note the nonskid rubber heel and sole with tap added to the basic character shoe.

MEN
Character Shoes
Ballet Shoes
Jazz Oxfords
Tap Shoes

WOMEN
Character Shoes
Ballet Shoes
Jazz Oxfords (Optional)
Tap Shoes
Pointe Shoes

Dancewear. Colors and styles of dancewear can accent your body line or detract from it to the point of showing up problem areas. If you are given a choice of what to wear, but have problems in deciding, then let a fellow dancer help. At times, it is hard to be objective, but with another person's opinion you can often get some insights about your appearance that you may not have had before. A friend can often observe you from a distance, and then make suggestions for change if a design or color combination makes you appear heavy or breaks the line of your body. The final decision should always be your own, but be conscientious enough to ask for a second opinion when in doubt.

Of course, the type of audition will often determine the type of dancewear. For a *ballet* audition, consider taking the following items:

WOMEN

Black Leotard. Styles vary in neckline and sleeve length, so pick the one that is flattering to your body line.

Pink Tights with Feet. Helpful Hint: cut the bottom seam on the feet of your tights so that, if you are asked to perform modern dance movements, you will be prepared to roll up the feet of the tights to the ankles.

(If the traditional style of leotards and tights is not required, pick a color and style that will look good on you and will give appropriate focus.)

Pink Ballet Slippers. Make sure you have elastic sewn on, and secure all bows inside the shoe while wearing them.

Pink Pointe Shoes. Sew on pink ribbons securely and bring lambs' wool with you. Also, carry an extra pair of pointe shoes for emergencies.

MEN

Black Tights with Feet. Cut the seam in the feet so that you can also use the tights for modern dance.

White Tank Top or Tank Shirt. If you wear a tank shirt, make sure you secure and smooth it in your tights to make a clean line.

Dancebelt. Despite the uncomfortable drawbacks, the dancebelt was designed to give the male dancer the line and additional support needed, and should never be confused with or substituted by an athletic supporter.

Black or White Ballet Shoes. You may wear white socks with your ballet shoes, but check with the company personnel handling the audition for specific requirements.

It would not hurt both male and female dancers to bring along extra pairs of leotards, tights, and shoes for emergencies. You may be carrying a lot of dancewear, but it is better to be ready for anything than to be caught unprepared. Often, the company that is giving the audition will post the required dancewear, but if they do not, a quick phone call can resolve a lot of worries.

For *Broadway, television,* or *show* auditions, women should wear leotards and light-colored beige tights or flesh-colored fishnet tights. Flesh-colored fishnet tights are very flattering to the legs in character shoes and are standard dancewear items for many professional shows. Wrap skirts are also acceptable for these types of auditions. Men should wear a leotard or tank top with jazz pants. They should not wear tights with jazz or character

Character shoes worn with tights tends to break the body line and make the dancer appear awkward.

shoes: tights tend to make the shoe look out of place as well as breaking the line of the body.

In *modern dance* auditions, the dancer usually may pick the style and color of leotards and tights. Wear a style that is flattering to the line of your body and avoid outrageous colors that may distort your body line. Modern auditions are usually done in bare feet, but there are a few variations. Some dancers wear tights without feet, others prefer stirrup tights. A few like using the modern sandal, which consists of a soft leather sole that is laced or strapped to the foot.

The only unacceptable items of clothing for any dance audition are baggy warmup clothes. They make it very difficult for the auditioner to see what type of line you have. Occasionally, an auditioner will allow you to wear additional clothing during the warmups if it is unusually cold. If in doubt . . . ask.

Now that you know some basic approaches to looking your best, let us consider other important impressions that should be made during an audition.

PERSONALITY

Each auditioner has his own mental list of impressions that a dancer has made during an audition. You can be sure that personality, professionalism, and discipline are at the top of his evaluation list. When I say personality, I do not only mean projection while you are dancing. It is very important for the choreographer to know if his dancers can work well with him, which usually means maintaining a pleasant attitude and disciplined working habits. Of course, you may think, "How can I ever convey that in an audition?" Many times you cannot, but consistency in attitude throughout the entire audition will undoubtedly be noticed.

Interview

If the auditioner is interested in you, he will often include an interview with your audition. If an interview is held, make sure you are pleasant, businesslike, and concise in answering all questions. Auditioners are not interested in hearing your life story. If asked about your qualifications, highlight only the best points. The night before an audition, it can be helpful to make a mental list of some questions that might be asked. Security about answering correctly will also instill extra confidence in your auditioning approach. Most of the questions will stem from your resume, so go over it thoroughly before handing a copy to the auditioner.

Some interview questions that might be asked are:

How many years have you danced?

Why did you audition for this particular company or show?

If offered the job, are you prepared to start immediately?

What do you consider your main strengths in dance?

Have you had any injuries or major illnesses?

Do you have references, or do you mind if we telephone your previous employer for a recommendation?

In what technique are you primarily trained?

Have you had partnering experience?

How long have you lived at your present address?

Why do you want to leave your present job?

How long have you been unemployed?

Have you seen our company perform? If so, what do you think of our company?

How did you hear about this job opening?

Do you have something prepared in your own style to show us?

What do you like to do in your spare time?

Do you mind touring?

On Stage

When it comes to personality on stage, remember to remain consistent throughout the entire audition. This means that your warmups as well as the dance combinations should possess qualities of performance. The auditioner is looking for disciplined dancers who are quick to learn; prepare yourself to pick up the combinations immediately so that you can give plenty of attention to layering the proper quality of performance on top of the movements. Do not just pace yourself through the steps, but give your all each time you approach a new combination. Also, limit your questions during the audition; the auditioner only has a certain amount of time and does not like to be distracted from his train of thought.

Colleagues

Dealing with other dancers' egos is part of the auditioning process wherever you go. At times, you will be subjected to the scrambling of dancers for the best possible place on stage. It is understandable in such a competitive situation. I am not saying that finding the best place to be seen is bad, but be courteous in your approach because it prevents a lot of tension. On the other hand, do not be pushed around. If someone happens to come into your space while dancing, stand your ground and do not let your concentration falter. Keep performing to your fullest and adjust to the situation.

There will also be times when you are confronted with auditioners who may be either unsettling or unencouraging. Although they may seem cold or cruel, realize that they are there for one purpose—to hire the best. Keep a pleasant attitude and good concentration, even during the worst moments of an audition.

All photographs by Douglas Mackenzie

If you are prepared physically and mentally from the moment you sign in . . . through the performance of the combinations . . . during evaluation and interviews . . . to the point of reorganizing for callbacks . . . you will have that added touch of confidence you need to excel in the auditioning process.

11

2

PROFESSIONAL RESUMES AND PORTFOLIOS

★★★★★★★★★★★★★★★★★★★★★★★★★★★★★★★★★★★★★★

RESUMES

One of the most valuable passports a dancer has when auditioning is his professional resume. The French word, "résumé," means "summary" and refers to a fact sheet that is used to identify, describe, and list qualifications of a person in terms of experience and education. A copy of the original and an 8" × 10" glossy headshot photograph are standard items given by the dancer to the prospective employer. There are several different approaches in making a well-organized and impressive resume, but before discussing formats, it is necessary to know some basic guidelines.

Preparation

Your resume should be no longer than *one* 8" × 10" page in length, with your glossy headshot photograph stapled on the reverse side. The content should be concise, clear in format, comprehensive, and neatly typed. Proofread the original and check for typewriter flaws, such as light and dark letters or incomplete printing of letters. Rather than chancing an old typewriter, find a professional typist to do the work on a high-quality typewriter. The copies can only be as good as your original.

Never use the original resume and photograph for an audition because they are not returned. Have plenty of copies on hand for future auditions. Professional typing and duplicating can be done fairly inexpensively if you shop around. The trade papers* advertise businesses that specialize in just this type of work. You can also check the Yellow Pages under the heading, Copying and Duplicating Service. If you need only a few copies from the original, use a Xerox machine. Extensive duplicating can be done by mimeographing, photocopying, multilith processing, or offset printing. Whatever method is used to reproduce your original, make sure it is done on good-quality paper.

Always keep your resume up to date. This is done in reverse chronological order, that is, list your most recent and most important experiences first. Do not forget to include any particular specialties you might have in your repertoire; you never know when a choreographer, director, or producer is looking for someone who can handle props, spit fire, and dance at the same time. Also remember to put your *present* address and telephone number on your resume. If you do not have a telephone, list an answering-service number. Many professional dancers and actors, who can not afford the answering service fees, invest in an answering-service machine that hooks up to their home telephone. It is a wonderful asset when you find that you are in and out a lot and have no one to answer the telephone for you.

Format

Before you choose a resume format, it may be valuable to examine a basic outline step by step in order to list all

---

*Newsstand publications that serve the communications and entertainment industries.

experiences, training, and other important data properly. Follow Sample Resume 1 on page 18.

Personal Data.   Place your name at the top center portion of the paper, leaving plenty of room below for headings. Type your name as you would like to have it seen printed in a program. At the left-side margin, below your name, type your telephone (or answering-service) number and address. Do not forget the area and zip codes. At the right-hand side, place a short personal data column, which is very helpful to the auditioner. This column usually states your height, weight, and color of hair and eyes. Your birthdate is optional, but including it here will save the trouble of being asked later. Some people prefer to give other data information, such as:

Voice: Baritone

Range: Low G to F above middle C

Age: 20-45 [Describes the age range of roles you can act]

Dancer/Actor/Singer: [Shows the order of your strengths]

As for padding the truth, my advice is not to take the chance. It is very hard to lie about certain things, such as height and weight, and your age can always be checked if the need arises. I have attended certain auditions where dancers were weighed and measured, so do not take the chance of being embarrassed by the auditioner because you stretched the truth too far.

Specializations.   After the personal data column, the rest of your resume will be divided into specific headings. Always categorize your resume so that your most impressive qualifications for the area in which you are interested appear first. For example, a performer lists performance experience first, then teaching and choreography. The same order of emphasis should be placed in applying for a teaching job: teaching experience first, followed by training, performing, and choreography.

Performance Experience may be your first heading. Often, dancers who are just out of college have no choice other than to list high-school and college performances until they gain more professional experience. Do not be embarrassed if you have to do this, but remember to eliminate these earlier experiences as your repertoire grows. The subheadings used under the major heading, *Performance Experience,* will greatly depend on the extent of your repertoire. Some appropriate examples are Theater Experience, Summer Stock Experience, Ballet Companies, Modern Dance Companies, Jazz Dance Companies, Community Theater Experience, Television Dancing, Film Experience and College Dance Experience. If you have had only one experience in an area, try to place it under a larger general heading.

Training is the next heading below *Performance Experience.* This list should include college and university degrees, conservatory training, private dance school training, or names of the instructors with whom you studied for an extended period of time. You may choose to list master classes with professional dancers or summer dance workshops, but limit them to those that were especially influential. Do not forget to put down dates: the month and year is usually sufficient for most of your entries.

Teaching Experience is the next heading on your resume. You may think that this heading is only for dancers who are looking for teaching jobs, but do not be mistaken. Teaching experience can be an important element of qualifications for a performing position. Many companies want their dancers to be able to teach master classes when the occasion arises. Your teaching services may further be required by a dance company that books touring residencies, summer workshops, or master classes for promotional purposes. Dancers who teach well will also be able to freelance during the off-season to earn extra money. If you are weak in this area, I suggest that you get some teaching experience immediately to help strengthen your resume. In this list, you should identify each entry by giving the place of employment, the title of the position, and the year(s). If there is space, also include what you taught.

Choreographic Experience is the next heading. If you intend to use this category on your resume, list all choreographic works under one general heading until your repertoire is extensive

16

enough to be subdivided into specific choreographies, such as ballet, modern, jazz, musical comedy, opera, television, film, choreography for dramas, show dance, or fashion show. These categories may be further subdivided into professional, community, summer stock, or college choreography. Each choreographic category should also have dates, unless you are listing numerous pieces and need the extra space.

Specialties is the last heading on your resume. These special abilities can be very useful in landing that long-awaited job. A choreographer for a musical may be interested in someone who can juggle as well as dance; some Las Vegas shows are interested in dancers who also have acrobatic and ice-skating experience. If you are proficient in other areas, especially those that would be an asset to your present career, list them under this heading. The following list focuses on some examples:

Gymnastics, tumbling, or acrobatics

Ice skating

Juggling

Mime

Fencing

Stage Combat

Musical Instruments [List only those that you play well]

Acting and singing [If you are a musical comedy dancer, these abilities should be listed under a separate heading]

Costuming, lighting, or scenic design

Dance specialties, such as tap, character dance, folk, or social forms

Directing [In summer stock, one person is often choreographer and director]

Samples.   The following pages of sample resumes are presented to give you a clearer understanding of different formats. Although there is a variety of samples to choose from, you will

SAMPLE RESUME 1
Comprehensive

MARGARET MASSON

Phone: (000) 000-0000

Address: 220 West 21st Street
           New York, N.Y. 00000

Height: 5'8"
Weight: 115
Eyes: Brown
Hair: Black
Birthdate: 4/14/50

PERFORMANCE EXPERIENCE

Dance Companies

Jose Limon Dance Company, New York, New York 1980
Repertory Dance Theatre, Salt Lake City, Utah 1976
Dance Alive, Gainesville, Florida 1975

Theatre Companies

Mule Barn Summer Theatre, Tarkio, Missouri 1978-80
Pioneer Memorial Theatre Company, Salt Lake City, Utah 1973

College Dance Companies

Orchesis, University of Utah, Salt Lake City 1972-74
Dance Consort, University of Florida, Gainesville 1971

DANCE EDUCATION

University of Utah, Salt Lake City: M.F.A. in Modern Dance 1974
University of Florida, Gainesville: B.F.A. in Dance 1972
High School for the Performing and Visual Arts, Houston, Texas
1965-68

TEACHING EXPERIENCE

Dance Coordinator, Glassboro State College, Glassboro,
    New Jersey 1977
Guest Artist, Ricks Fine Arts Summer Academy, Rexburg,
    Idaho 1973

CHOREOGRAPHY EXPERIENCE [If space permits, include the names of
companies for which the works were done]

Choreodramas, Modern and Jazz Choreography

Six Wives of Henry VIII 1976, Transformations 1976, Six
Statements 1975, The Guardians 1974, Lady of the Snow 1974

Ballets and Operas

Nutcracker 1976, Sleeping Beauty 1976, Coppelia 1975,
Carmina Burana 1972, Die Fledermaus 1972, Carmen 1971,
Salome 1971

Musicals and Plays with Choreography

West Side Story 1979, Kismet 1979, Kiss Me Kate 1979,
Brigadoon 1978, Cabaret 1978, Anything Goes 1977,
Music Man 1977

SPECIALTIES

Tap   Mime   Stage Combat

SAMPLE RESUME 2

Sample 1 altered to meet audition description: "Female modern dancer needed for small modern company. Must also be able to choreograph for company's repertory."

MARGARET MASSON

Phone: (000) 000-0000

Address: 220 West 21st Street
            New York, N.Y. 00000

Height: 5'8"
Weight: 115
Eyes: Brown
Hair: Black
Birthdate: 4/14/50

PERFORMANCE EXPERIENCE

   Professional Dance Companies

      Jose Limon Dance Company, New York, New York 1980

      Repertory Dance Theatre, Salt Lake City, Utah 1976

      Dance Alive, Gainesville, Florida 1975

   Summer Stock Companies

      Mule Barn Summer Theatre, Tarkio, Missouri 1978-80

      Pioneer Memorial Theatre Company, Salt Lake City, Utah 1973

CHOREOGRAPHY EXPERIENCE

   Modern Dance

      Transformations Dance Alive, Gainesville, Florida 1975
      Lady of the Snow Dance Alive, Gainesville, Florida 1975
      Six Statements Ricks Fine Arts Summer Academy, Rexburg,
                  Idaho 1973
      The Guardians Ricks Fine Arts Summer Academy, Rexburg,
                  Idaho 1973

   Ballets and Operas

      List upon request

   Musical Theatre

      List upon request

DANCE EDUCATION

      University of Utah, Salt Lake City: M.F.A. in Modern Dance 1974
      University of Florida, Gainesville: B.F.A. in Dance 1972
      High School for the Performing and Visual Arts, Houston, Texas
      1965-68

TEACHING EXPERIENCE

      Glassboro State College, Dance Coordinator, Glassboro,
         New Jersey 1977
      Ricks Fine Arts Summer Academy, Guest Artist, Rexburg,
         Idaho 1973

SAMPLE RESUME 3

Musical Theater
[Confirmation of credentials can be done through the agency and unions,
which allows for simplification of the resume]

AEA-SAG-AFTRA

Robert Duva Management
(000) 000-0000
Service
(000) 000-0000

Height: 5'7"
Weight: 120
Eyes: Blue
Hair: Black
[Birthdate is often
excluded]

BROADWAY	DANCIN' (Original Broadway Cast, Director: Bob Fosse)
	A CHORUS LINE (Original Broadway Cast, Director: Michael Bennett)
	PIPPIN (Original Broadway Cast, Director: Bob Fosse)
TOURS	MAME (with Angela Lansbury)
	GYPSY ("Tulsa")
	WEST SIDE STORY ("Arab")
TELEVISION	THE BARBARA MANDRELL SHOW (Featured performer/NBC)
	THE RAQUEL WELCH SPECIAL (ABC)
	THE LYNDA CARTER SPECIAL (CBS)
NIGHTCLUB	SOLO NIGHTCLUB ACT (Reno Sweeney's, New York City)
REGIONAL THEATRE	HARVEY; OKLAHOMA; THE KING AND I; BRIGADOON; SHOWBOAT; FIDDLER ON THE ROOF; PROMISES, PROMISES; MUSIC MAN; KISS ME KATE
INDUSTRIAL	MILLIKEN; OLDSMOBILE; BUICK; PEPSI COLA
COMMERCIALS	List upon request
CHOREOGRAPHY	List upon request
SPECIAL SKILLS	Water and Snow Skiing, Scuba Diving, Roller Skating

SAMPLE RESUME 4
Musical Theater—Narrative Form

Phone: (000) 000-0000
Address: 13 West 26th Street
New York, N.Y. 00000

MARK HOLLIS

DANCER/CHOREOGRAPHER/DIRECTOR

Birthdate 5/6/50; 6'11"; 150 pounds; blue eyes; brown hair

Performance Experience `

Summer 1982-1983	Director and choreographer for the Waldo-Astoria Dinner Theater, Kansas City, Missouri. Duties also included performing in the production of <u>Kiss Me Kate</u> and <u>Brigadoon</u>.
September 1981-April 1982	Toured with the National Touring Company of <u>Music Man</u> for approximately twenty-four weeks. Promoted to dance captain after the first six weeks of touring.
1978-1981	Performed for the past three years in a bus and truck tour of <u>Rodgers and Hart</u>, a musical revue performed in the New England states.

Education

1975-1978	Trained at the Clark Center in New York City as a dancer and choreographer. Specialized in jazz and tap.
1972-1975	B.F.A. in Theatre, 1975, Directing emphasis, Ohio State University, Columbus.
References	Available upon request

21

SAMPLE RESUME 5
Ballet

SARAH   KNERR

SAG-AFTRA-AGMA

Home: (000) 000-0000   Light Brown Hair
Service: (000) 000-0000   Green Eyes
                                                   5'3"
                                                   100 lbs.

<u>AMERICAN BALLET THEATRE</u> (Soloist 1976-1983)

    THE NUTCRACKER   THEME AND VARIATIONS
    GISELLE   DON QUIXOTE ("Amour")
    FANCY FREE   LES SYLPHIDES
    THE SLEEPING BEAUTY ("Bluebird")   SACRE DU PRINTEMPS
    CONCERTO   AIRS
    COPPELIA   SWAN LAKE

<u>JOFFREY BALLET</u> (Soloist 1973-1976)

    SCOTCH SYMPHONY   INTERPLAY
    CAKEWALK   PINEAPPLE POLL
    TRINITY   DEUCE COUPE
    OPUS JAZZ   KETTENTANZ

<u>TELEVISION</u>

    THE NUTCRACKER
    LIVE FROM LINCOLN CENTER
    LIVE FROM ART PARK

<u>FILM</u>

    THE TURNING POINT (Featured)

<u>TRAINING</u>

    DANCE: American Ballet Theatre
            Joffrey Ballet
            Dayton Ballet Company, Dayton, Ohio

    ACTING: Bob McAndrew, New York City

    VOICE: Ora Witte, New York City

    MIME: Pilar Garcia, New York City

<u>COMMERCIALS</u> List upon request

22

SAMPLE RESUME 6
Ballet

```
                        Rodger Dodger
                        Phone: (000) 000-0000
                        Address: 2300 W. Powell
                                 San Francisco, CA 00000
```

DANCE EXPERIENCE

1980-   San Francisco Ballet -- Principal Dancer

                Romeo and Juliet ("Tybalt")
                Tarantella (Lead Dancer)
                Cinderella ("Stepsister")
                Firebird ("Prince Ivan")

1978-1980   Ballet West, Salt Lake City, Utah -- Principal Dancer

                Nutcracker ("The Prince")
                Sleeping Beauty ("Bluebird")
                Carmina Burana (Principal Dancer)
                Prince Igor ("Prince Igor")
                Swan Lake ("Prince Siegfried")

Summer 1979 Pioneer Memorial Theatre, Salt Lake City, Utah --
             Dancer/Actor

                Brigadoon ("Harry Beaton")
                Seesaw (Chorus dancer)
                Music Man ("Tommy")

TRAINING

1973-1977   Ballet Department, University of Utah, Salt Lake City:
             B.F.A. 1977

1970-1973   Rowland Butler: Tap and Jazz

AFFILIATIONS

1982   SAG/AFTRA

1980   AGMA

HOBBIES

Ice Skating   Juggling   Pen and Ink Drawing

PERSONAL

Height: 6'1"   Weight: 150   Eyes: Blue   Hair: Blond
               Birthdate: February 27, 1955

SAMPLE RESUME 7
Modern Dance

JANE WALLACE

Contact: (000) 000-0000
8801 University Street
New York, N.Y. 00000

PERFORMANCE EXPERIENCE

1978–   The Alvin Ailey American Dance Theater,
         New York, New York

Choreographic Work	Choreographer
Satyriade	Alvin Ailey
The Lark Ascending	Alvin Ailey
Revelations	Alvin Ailey
Rainbow 'Round My Shoulder	Donald McKayle
How Long Have It Been	Marlene Furtick
Missa Brevis	Jose Limon
The Wedding	Pearl Primus
Blues Suite	Alvin Ailey
Creation of the World	Alvin Ailey
Gillespiana	Alvin Ailey

1972–1978   Repertory Dance Theatre, Salt Lake City, Utah

Choreographic Work	Choreographer
Tin Tal	Bill Evans
Scarf Dance	Ruth St. Denis
Lyric Suite	Anna Sokolow
Nocturne	Donald McKayle
Three Promenades to the Lord	John Butler
Fatal Birds	Paul Sanasardo
Relief	Douglas Dunn
For Betty	Bill Evans
When Summoned	Bill Evans

TRAINING   North Carolina School of the Arts, Winston Salem:
                B.F.A. 1972

HONORS AND AWARDS   Graduated with high honors from North Carolina
                School of the Arts 1972

                Scholarship recipient, Repertory Dance Theatre's
                Summer Workshop 1970

PERSONAL

   Birthdate: April 7, 1950   Height: 5'11"   Weight: 140
                    Eyes: Brown   Hair: Black

24

find that they all have several elements in common. As you examine each sample, select some of the topic headings that would best represent your work. Do not be afraid to be creative in developing your resume. It is an advertisement for you; you want it to be appealing to the eye and effective in correctly stating all the facts. Since a great deal of thought must go into compiling a resume, take the time to make several work sheets before typing the final copy. Find an acceptable outline that can be easily updated after every job. Please remember: the purpose of the resume is to show a prospective employer a concise, clear, and neatly typed fact sheet of your qualifications. Do not leave for an audition without one.

PORTFOLIOS

Portfolios are used by professionals in a variety of careers as a means of showing examples of their work to prospective employers. A choreographer, producer, or director will frequently ask to see your portfolio during an interview. Unlike the resume, a portfolio is your own personal companion that is never given out permanently. Not only is it a useful device to sell yourself, but an important file to refer to when you need copies of original recommendations, your resume, or reviews.

There are various formats in organizing your portfolio, but remember to be clear and to the point. Do not confuse a scrapbook with a portfolio, which is not used for the purpose of accumulating an abundance of dance mementos, but serves to display the dancer in his best work.

Format

A professional portfolio should include the original resume, an 8″ × 10″ glossy headshot photograph, performance photographs, reviews, programs, and recommendations. Accumulating the appropriate materials and organizing them well are of prime importance. Following are some suggestions for creating a professional portfolio.

Materials. Start by placing everything in one file. From this, select the best and most impressive pieces and put them in a

A professional portfolio is well organized and highlights an artist's best work.

large, three-ring binder. The binder should be a solid color: covers with animals, flowers, or extravagant designs do not look professional. The material you place inside the binder should be protected with transparent plastic covers, which can be purchased in most stationery stores. Many dancers like to use the first two pages to show their original resume and 8" × 10" glossy headshot.

Programs.

Reviews. Favorable reviews of your artistic achievements are very valuable additions to your portfolio and should be underlined in the same manner as the programs. If you have a lengthy newspaper or magazine review that deals entirely with your work, take the time to edit it by underlining only the important parts.

You may often overlook reviews unless you keep your eyes peeled for them. Sometimes, you will know when a review is to be printed and can watch the papers for it. At other times, you will have to depend on friends or employers who have seen the review to alert you or to give you a copy. If all else fails, write down the date and name of the publication and purchase a back issue or make a Xerox from the library's copy. Most dance company publicity managers are helpful in locating a copy if you have the correct information. One of their duties is to keep files of reviews.

Recommendations. Letters of recommendation are significant additions to a portfolio. You should try to accumulate them from employers, instructors, and artists who have a good insight into your ability. In making your decision about which letters to include, pick only those that are well written and concise. They must be signed, with the signatory clearly identified. For example:

> Sincerely,
>
> [Signature]
>
> John Doe
> Artistic Director of The Dallas
> Repertory Ballet Theatre

or

> Best regards,
>
> [Signature]
>
> John Henry
> Dance Department Chairman
> University of Florida

Whenever possible, choose recommendations typed on letter-head stationery. If you come across a letter you want to use, but it lacks appropriate identification, by all means type the identification and staple it to the letter.

The appropriate placement of your recommendations in the portfolio is a matter of choice. You may either group your letters together or insert them under the various headings that correspond to specific jobs or experience, for example, place letters of recommendation from summer-stock directors and choreographers with programs, photographs, and reviews from that season's repertoire. Recommendations should be updated from time to time, so do not hesitate to add new ones to your portfolio.

Photographs. A variety of good-quality photographs is highly recommended for a dancer's portfolio. In addition to a resume photograph, a selection of action shots is needed to give the reader some idea of how you look in performance. Posed, full-length shots should be included, as well, to reveal your body line. Usually, a dance company or show will hire a photographer to take shots of concerts or particular performances for publicity purposes. The photographer will often post a "contact sheet" for company dancers who are interested in purchasing pictures. This person is an excellent source for very good copies of performance photographs. Since this is a means for him to earn extra money, he is usually more than willing to duplicate, for a fee, any shots in the size that you wish. He may also be willing to take a solo shot of you in your costume. Do not be afraid to ask, if you need additional photographs.

Although black and white glossies are standard, always try to purchase color slides as well, which you can use as negatives to develop additional photographs. If you cannot purchase slides, ask for the negatives. Even if some professional photographers refuse to sell the negatives for fear of losing additional duplicating purchases, others will gladly sell them to you with your photographs. It does not hurt to ask. All slides and negatives should be kept in a safe place, not in your portfolio.

The resume photograph is the most important one in your portfolio, since the copies of that particular shot are given out permanently for auditioners' files. As it is the one advertising photograph that has to sell you each time there is an audition, make sure it is the best one. If it is done professionally, a nice

Wayne Cilento/Auditioners sometimes request a full-length action photograph in addition to your headshot. Make sure you have a good selection from which to choose, or invest in a composite (over), which shows your headshot and several full-length dance shots.

Eric Brandt Nielsen.

Barbara Hanks/ A variety of headshots allows for choice aimed at the specific type of audition.

option is to have your name printed at the bottom. Avoid wearing heavy makeup for your headshot.

Less expensive than having a professional photographer take studio shots is to ask friends who are amateur photographers to help you with your resume photograph and a selection of full-length photographs. The quality is often just as good. Occasionally, you can arrange for your friends to take photographs during dress rehearsals. It also helps if they can see an entire run-through before shooting. Better photographs are taken when the photographer is familiar with the movements that a dancer is about to execute and if he knows exactly where that dancer is going to be on stage at any given moment. Also, do not forget to ask your friends to take individual posed shots of you in costume. Anticipate the individual shots that you will need, then have them taken on stage after the rehearsal or in front of an appropriately lighted backdrop.

Professional studio photographers can give you not only a choice of posed shots with the type of body line that you want to show, but the best photo quality. The photographs taken at a studio are usually much clearer in detail because of the sophisticated equipment and ample setup time for each shot. Of course, you will pay more for this type of service; the better the photographer, the more expensive each copy will be. Diversification in your portfolio is a must, so select the best shots of yourself in a variety of choreographic works and styles.

Other Formats

Often dancers who are being interviewed by a search committee for a teaching job or guest-artist position will present their portfolio in the form of a slide or videotape show. This is an excellent way to show off your work in a visually exciting and well-organized manner. The only dangers in this approach are a too lengthy format and lack of proper equipment at the site of your interview. If you decide to present a slide show or videotape, make sure your interviewers know ahead of time that you will need special equipment. You may invest in your own equipment, but you will be faced with the problem of carrying it around with you. Above all, edit the slides or videotape carefully so that only the best points of your work are highlighted.

Alternatives to a portfolio in job interviews include slide shows and videotapes.

3

ADJUSTING TO CITY LIFE

★★

The move from a sheltered training environment to a major population center is addressed by a professional dancer who has solved part of the problem by combining dance studio and living quarters.

LAURA GLENN

Dancer-choreographer. Formerly a featured soloist with the José Limón Dance Company. Toured extensively, and has restaged Limón and Doris Humphrey works on companies around the world. She and her husband, Gary Lund, founded and direct their own company, Glenn•Lund•Dance.

Many young dancers experience a tremendous cultural shock when moving into a new city after graduating from a university, dance school, or conservatory. A dancer's approach to being thoroughly prepared for the auditioning process can be initiated properly only after he is settled in his new environment. Dancers can get so discouraged just by the magnitude of the city that they lose sight of their career objectives. On the other hand, trying to take the city by storm can be just as defeating.

35

J. Elbers

Laura Glenn and Gary Lund in Rivet

The dancer has to find a niche that is right for him and participate in city life.

A dancer has to be hooked on the art form in a spiritual way to make it through the rough times. I am not just talking about New York. Give yourself time coming into a big city. Do not be quick to say yes to anything. Treat the city like a cafeteria; know that you eyes are bigger than your stomach.

[Like so many artists I interviewed, Laura Glenn does not recommend a major city for those who are indecisive about what they want.] I play the devil's advocate when lecturing on the lifestyle of a dancer in New York by painting a glum picture for the student, especially as a modern dancer, since the financial benefits are always limited. They need to want to come to New York without any illusions. If I cannot discourage them, then I know they are the ones who should come to the city. If they have the desire to try to make a career in New York, they should definitely take the chance, always keeping in mind why they are there, so that they are not swallowed up by the competitive and teeming environment.

If a dancer is planning to move to New York, I recommend a booklet entitled, *Poor Dancer's Almanac, A Guide to Living and Dancing in New York*. [A new and updated 300-page edition has recently been published by Dance Theater Workshop, 219 West 19th Street, New York, NY 10011. The booklet includes housing needs, health needs, dance organization publications, financial needs, taxes and record keeping, and even entertainment suggestions.] There are also many guidebooks and maps published on New York city life, which can be found in most bookstores. I highly recommend that you invest in a few of these guidebooks and bone up on them before moving to the city.

In addition to the information in guidebooks, the following is a list of suggestions that I hope will help the dancer prepare for city life.

First of all, you want to find a comfortable apartment, which will undoubtedly take some time. It would be wise to bring enough money to live reasonably for several months. If you can stay with friends or sublet at first, it can be a tremendous help. Friends can also suggest good neighborhoods, and roommates are highly recommended as a means of gathering information and keeping in touch with what is going on in the city. Do not accept what appears to be a "good deal" in a rough or dangerous neighborhood: it may not be as good as you think. After considering transportation—the accessibility of subways or trains, or the cost of taxis to and from your apartment to the studio and your job in order to feel safe—you may find that "good deal" apartment not as beneficial as expected.

Know your other marketable talents. You have to support yourself during the auditioning process or periods of unemployment. A job that relates to your career is helpful, when available. Examples of jobs that dancers take are arts administration, stage management, lighting, typing, operating a computer, writing advertisement copy, sewing, baby sitting, house cleaning, and waiting tables. Find a job that gives you time to take classes and is flexible enough to allow adjustment of hours in case a performing job is accepted.

Once you are somewhat settled and taking classes, listen with patience and intelligence, in dressing rooms and studios for information about auditions. Keep in touch with instructors and friends in the arts with whom you have studied or worked who may relay news about an audition. Classes, workshops, or summer festivals (like the American Dance Festival or Jacob's Pillow) will also expose you to many people and large faculties who may prove good contacts.

Bear in mind that you must know how to budget your money month to month, but also that there are necessary indulgences to make you feel better from week to week— reading books or going to a health spa. Awareness of your resources will help you achieve this end.

Your body is a sensitive instrument which you must care for constantly. How you protect your body depends on the hours you give it. Your diet and choice of clothing for city life are important. Even footwear. I cannot believe some of the uncomfortable and impractical shoes that dancers choose to wear in a city where walking is a major means of transportation. Take care of your body! There are periods when you should be wild—splurge on a new outfit or treat yourself to something you crave—but know what is best in the long view. Be sensible.

4

THEATRICAL DANCE AUDITIONS

★★★★★★★★★★★★★★★★★★★★★★★★★★★★★★★★★★★★

This chapter focuses on Broadway, industrial, television and film, and Las Vegas show auditioning. Professional insights are given by the following choreographers and dancers.

WAYNE CILENTO
Broadway and film dancer, singer, and actor
Dancin'—Dancer/Singer/Actor in original cast
The Act—Dancer/Singer/Actor in original cast
Chorus Line—Dancer/Singer/Actor in original cast

BARBARA HANKS
Sugar Babies—Originated the role of "Sally Rand"
Oh, Kay!—Dancer/Singer/Actress
Perfectly Frank—Assistant choreographer/Dancer

GEOFFREY HOLDER
Broadway, television, film choreographer, director, dancer, and actor
Annie (film)—Actor
Timbuktu—Director, choreographer and costume designer
The Wiz—Director and costume designer

ADRIAN LE PELTIER

Assistant company manager, dance captain, and dancer
Hello Hollywood Hello—Assistant Company Manager
M.G.M. Grand Hotel
Reno, Nevada
Chesterfield, Repertory Theatre—Performer
Chesterfield, Derbyshire, England
Latin Quarter—Performer
London, England

HENRY LE TANG

Tap choreographer and instructor
Sophisticated Ladies—Tap choreographer
Eubie—Choreographer
Crazy in the Heat—Choreographer

TOMMY PEEL

Television and nightclub dancer
Ann-Margret Show—Dance captain
Raw Satin—Performer
Donny and Marie Show—Dancer

DENNY SHEARER

Broadway choreographer and dancer
Annie (film)—Assistant choreographer
Music Is—Assistant choreographer
American Dance Machine—Dancer/Singer/Actor

TONY STEVENS

Broadway, television, film choreographer and dancer
Best Little Whorehouse in Texas (film)—Choreographer
Spotlight—Choreographer
Mary Tyler Moore Show—Choreographer

LEE THEODORE

Artistic director and founder of the American Dance Machine.
Broadway, television, film choreographer and dancer
West Side Story—Originated Broadway role of "Anybodys"
West Side Story—Director and choreographer of the Lincoln Center revival in 1968
Song of Norway—Film choreographer

TOMMY TUNE

Broadway director, choreographer, and dancer
My One and Only—1983 Tony Award winner/Best choreographer and actor in a musical
Nine—1982 Tony Award winner/Best director
Cloud 9—Director/Obie Drama Desk Award winner
Best Little Whorehouse in Texas—Co-director and choreographer
A Day in Hollywood/A Night in the Ukraine—Tony Award winner/Best choreographer

CHARLES WARD

Broadway, film, and former American Ballet Theatre dancer
Staying Alive (film)—Featured Actor/Dancer ("Butler")
Dancin'—Dancer/Singer/Actor in original cast
American Ballet Theatre—Soloist
Turning Point—Dancer/Actor

Show business is one of the most dreamt-about careers, one which usually evokes images of glamour and stardom. Unfortunately, few obtain the "star" category; today's performing artists are more frequently seen in unemployment than onstage lines. This is due mainly to the precarious existence of any production. So many shows open and close yearly and so many television or film roles are only one-time occurrences that dancers in show business become the most professional auditionees around. Still, with all the pitfalls and high odds, the excitement of working with exceptional, creative choreographers and associating with other professional dancers makes even a short-lived career in show business well worth the effort.

THE GYPSY

The word "gypsy" used to be a popular label for a chorus dancer. However, the term is quickly fading in the show-business world of today. Tony Stevens has explained, "A gypsy used to be a dancer who was satisfied with a career of going from one show to another as a chorus member. Today, gypsy dancers do not exist as we once knew them, especially on Broadway." He feels that economic necessity has transformed the gypsy into a well-

A Little Night Music *at the Mule Barn Summer Theatre, Tarkio, Missouri.*

Paul Hustoles

rounded performer who also acts and sings. There are no longer the budgets for a chorus of singers, a chorus of dancers, and a full cast of actors. The multitalented performer is continually sought and the "triple-threat competitor" (one who acts, sings, and dances) has forced or frightened many dancers out of this field.

Geoffrey Holder contends that, "The auditioners of today have to cast a chorus of prospective stars, for those chorus members are also chosen to become the understudies for leads in the show." It is not uncommon for chorus members to attain their first big break this way. Because illness and injury are always a threat to productions that have extensive runs, understudies are depended upon greatly to cover emergencies.

Quite a few dancers and choreographers, who originally considered themselves gypsies, have experienced the transition to today's dancer. Some smile while others shudder at the new demands. Talented gypsies, like Tony Stevens, Denny Shearer, and Wayne Cilento, soon became dissatisfied with just being chorus members and found the addition of singing and acting to be much more stimulating and marketable for their careers. Dancers who have had troubles adapting to changing demands have either found instructors for additional training or changed careers.

Because the chorus dancer now has to act and sing, there is more opportunity for his career to branch off into other areas of performance, especially when the physical demands of dancing can no longer be met. Greater diversity also gives the dancer that extra confidence needed for singer-dancer or even singer-actor auditions. Today, it is imperative to have as much theater arts instruction as possible.

TRAINING

General

Although the training of a dancer who wishes to go into show business can be accomplished in various ways, I believe that the most beneficial foundation for developing a variety of skills is

Denny Shearer/The transition of the gypsy dancer to a multitalented performer who dances, sings, and acts, is seen in his career. He also has expanded his choreographic talents into film, television, and Broadway.

obtained in a conservatory, college, or university setting. In such programs, a dancer can gain comprehensive and diversified training with a group of instructors who are not only specialized in different dance areas, but who work collectively in evaluating and developing his growth. This provides a more cohesive understanding for the dancer as well as furnishing him with a degree to fall back on in the future. I am convinced that dancers have an ideal opportunity to develop as well-rounded artists under the umbrella of higher education. The exposure to the areas of performance, choreography, and teaching and the opportunity to train in related theater arts are invaluable.

Talented young dancers who are eager to start out immediately from high school should have a solid foundation of dance, acting, and voice training before they even consider a show-business career. If they lack these skills, they will eventually pay more for them. Barbara Hanks has disclosed some of her misgivings about her training. She somewhat sadly says, "One thing I regretted about my college education was the fact that I did not take more advantage of my vocal training while I was there." She now confesses that she spends hundreds of dollars a year for vocal training, which could have been acquired along with her college dance classes.

Dance

A dancer must continue dance training throughout his career. The growth and experience of a professional dancer in show business is not only established by stage performance, but through constant awareness of how to keep the instrument, the body, in top condition. Only through persistent training can that be achieved. Even for dancers who work nightly, technique classes are a part of their working schedule.

Ballet. An excellent foundation for developing body placement, line, stretch, and strength.

Lee Theodore says, "Your ballet training must be continued. You must realize that once you have the technique, it just does not stop there. From eight pirouettes, there is always eleven and from entrechat-six there is entrechat-huit. There is always something more to strive for." Wayne Cilento adds, "I myself am going back to ballet to continue my training and improve my technique. Besides that, a dancer will look better in jazz dance if he has classical training." While providing a solid basic technique, ballet is not the only form a show-business dancer must know.

Jazz. An important dance form that should be studied whenever possible. Dancers should start jazz in their teens because the sensualness that is so much a part of it can best be handled with growing maturity.

Jazz dance in West Side Story *at the Mule Barn Summer Theatre, Tarkio, Missouri.*

Paul Hustoles

Jazz is very popular because its rhythms, styles, and music relate to today's social-dance trends. Prime examples of musicals with jazz dance are *Dancin'*, *Chicago*, *A Chorus Line*, *The Wiz*, *Pippin*, *West Side Story*, and *Sweet Charity*.

Tap. This form will give the dancer invaluable training in rhythmic analysis and coordination. It has had a tremendous comeback on Broadway and is being incorporated in many auditions.

Henry Le Tang says, "Tap is back on Broadway and dancers have to realize that they have to get back in the factory and work for more than just a *time step*. I think I even convinced Judith Jamison, one of my dancers in *Sophisticated Ladies*, that she should take more tap." Memorable tap shows include *Sophisticated Ladies*, *Sugar Babies*, *42nd Street*, *Dames at Sea*, *No, No Nannette*, *George M*, and *Anything Goes*.

Social Dance. The social-dance forms in show business are undoubtedly the most widely used, whether they are in musicals, television, film, or even Las Vegas show dancing. They range from the waltz and jitterbug to disco and Latin forms.

Dancers can receive the experience of social dance through ballroom dance classes or first-hand experience in the shows themselves. Some musicals that include social-dance forms are *Cabaret* and *The Boyfriend* (Charleston); *West Side Story*, *Grease*, and *Bye Bye Birdie* (dances of the 1950s); and *My Fair Lady*, *Hello Dolly* and *A Little Night Music* (waltzes). One memorable show which had a very short run on Broadway but ran the gamut of social-dance forms was Michael Bennett's *Ballroom*.

Ethnic and Folk Dance. These dances are occasionally required in certain shows. A dancer usually obtains this experience from a folk-dance class or from the show itself.

Musicals that use these forms of dance include *Fiddler on the Roof*, *Brigadoon*, *Zorba*, *The King and I*, and *Kismet*. Of course, most musicals use more than one form of dancing. Cole Porter's *Kiss Me Kate* is an excellent example: there is jazz, tap, ballet, soft shoe, and even court dancing.

Henry Le Tang.

Social dance in My Fair Lady *at the Mule Barn Summer Theatre, Tarkio, Missouri.*

Acrobatics. Acrobatics, or basic gymnastics, often comes in handy for certain shows. Cartwheels, somersaults, flips, and walkovers are accomplishments that may place you in a better-paying specialty role. Of course, a dancer should not have to worry about anything beyond the basics. If the choreographer wants skilled acrobatics, he will hire an acrobat.

Michael Kidd is one choreographer who does place a great deal of emphasis on acrobatics in his choreography. One only has to look at a few of his shows, such as *The Music Man* or *Seven Brides for Seven Brothers,* to see how much he likes to use acro-dancing. If you go to one of his auditions, you should expect to be asked to show a few acrobatic skills. "Once, I auditioned for Michael Kidd," Lee Theodore says with a grin. "Everyone knows how big Michael is on acrobatics in his choreography. Well, in this audition he asked the dancers to do cartwheels. I still

51

Photographs by Paul Hustoles

Stylized ethnic dance forms in Brigadoon *and* Kismet *at the Mule Barn Summer Theatre, Tarkio, Missouri.*

remember coming up and saying to him, 'I am a dancer, not an acrobat, Mr. Kidd.' He politely responded by saying, 'Thank you, Lee,' and I was dismissed from the audition. That taught me a lesson I will not forget!"

Partnering. An important part of a dancer's training is learning how to partner and gaining experience in how to lift or be lifted. Comprehensive adagio, or partnering, classes are usually offered in ballet studios and schools.

Laura Quinn and Eric Nielsen demonstrate partnering.

Douglas Mackenzie

Many callbacks in auditioning will involve matching dancers and having them partner or execute certain lifts. Unfortunately, the female dancer is more vulnerable in this situation because she is required to convey the right body line while being lifted by the male dancer who is concealed behind her.

I have mentioned that a conservatory, college, or university program is excellent training for dancers interested in show business. Another valuable approach is to find a reputable instructor in a studio or school who will *teach* and not just *give* you the necessary dance forms. My biggest criticism of those teaching dance classes in private studios is that many just deliver a class to a student without explanation of technique, theory, or basic qualities of movement. Beware of these instructors, especially for those of you whose proper training requires extra attention. Also, be aware that the most popular dance classes are not necessarily the best. Popular dance classes are very crowded, which limits the available space as well as your ability to see the instructor's demonstrations and his ability to give personal attention.

I recommend that dancers study with several different instructors before devoting their time and money to any one studio or school. It is helpful to acquire information by word of mouth from other dancers. Since dancers are always searching for new, exciting, and highly recommended instructors, acquaint yourself with fellow classmates in order to keep up with the latest news.

UNIONS

Most auditions in New York City are "Equity," and unless a dancer belongs to the Actors' Equity Association and has a card in hand, he cannot be admitted to the audition. Actors' Equity does require Equity shows to hold open calls for nonmembers, but casting opportunities in these open calls are quite slim because selections have often been completed in the Equity auditions.

In order to become a member of Actors' Equity, you must either earn full Equity status or be cast in an Equity show, usually by means of an open call. Many dancers earn their Equity status by doing summer stock or dinner theater in houses with Equity apprenticeships. This is an excellent way for those just starting out to gain invaluable experience and important contacts for the future. Dancers who desire musical theater employment exclusively in New York should place an Equity card on their priority list of career goals. Without it, the auditioning process will not only be very limiting, but will become a major frustration.

On the other hand, before you rush to join a union, realize that there are many job opportunities throughout the United States that are nonunion. I would look closely at what you want and need out of a union card before getting one. It is a judgment that you have to make for yourself. There are other unions besides Actors' Equity in the world of show business from which you may purchase a membership card, depending on your need.

Every union represents dancers in various capacities. For further information concerning membership you should contact your local office, which is listed in your telephone book. If there is no local representative, address the main office.

ACTORS' EQUITY ASSOCIATION (AEA)
165 West 46th Street
New York, NY 10036
(212) 869-8530

Protects the rights and enforces rules of equity for dancers, actors, and singers in live musical theater and dramatic productions throughout the United States.

AMERICAN FEDERATION OF TELEVISION AND RADIO ARTISTS (AFTRA)
1350 Avenue of the Americas
New York, NY 10019
(212) 265-7700

Represents and protects performers in live and taped television and radio. It also represents performers in phonograph recording.

AMERICAN GUILD OF MUSICAL ARTISTS (AGMA)
1841 Broadway
New York, NY 10023
(212) 265-3687

Protects the rights of concert dancers and operatic and instrumental artists.

AMERICAN GUILD OF VARIETY ARTISTS (AGVA)
1540 Broadway
New York, NY 10036
(212) 765-0800

Protects the contractual rights of performers in live variety entertainment. Includes dancers, nightclub performers, and even animal acts.

SCREEN ACTORS' GUILD
All local offices are under the two main headquarters:
West Coast Office:
7750 Sunset Boulevard
Hollywood, CA 90046
(213) 876-3030

East Coast Office:
1700 Broadway
18th Floor
New York, NY 10019
(212) 876-5370

Represents and has jurisdiction over all performers (including dancers, under special circumstances) in the film medium. This includes television, movies, and some commercials.

Privileges and Benefits

The following fact sheet lists a few of the privileges and benefits provided by the unions just mentioned.

Access to union auditions is one of the dancer's most important privileges after he receives his union card.

The unions negotiate for higher wages and better working conditions for all their members.

They protect the interests and handle the complaints of union members concerning employment contracts.

They provide comprehensive health and pension plans.

They provide updated lists and newsletters on employment opportunities and union activities. Lists of advertising agencies, independent casting directors, and producers are also printed.

Many local unions as well as the main headquarters publish a talent directory. This is given to casting people in every phase of the entertainment world and contains the union member's picture and, usually, his address, telephone number, union affiliations, agent, and credits.

"Unfair lists" are also compiled and printed by many local and national union headquarters to protect their members from unfair practices by employers who have breached union contracts. Examples are producers who have not paid scale (minimum union) wages, delinquent payment of wages, or persistence in breaching union working hours. Union members may not accept employment from any prospective employer named on this list.

Green Rooms (Union Lounges) are usually provided both by local and national headquarters. They include a bulletin board with various information, copies of trade papers, and a place to relax and talk to fellow union members.

Fees

Each union requires its members to pay an initiation fee in addition to dues, which are often semi-annual. A dancer cannot receive a union card entitling him to the privileges of the union until these fees are paid. This can run to several hundred dollars, so be prepared for this expense if you are offered a contract in a union house. Fees are based on local or national representation.

Those who are working under the jurisdiction of one union often have the privilege of joining other unions at a lower fee. The interchangeability of union membership, an agreement among all the unions, gives the dancer an opportunity to work with protection in various union houses and in various performing circumstances. The only major drawback is the expense, especially for a dancer who has several union memberships but is not getting regular employment from these affiliations.

AUDITIONS

How Do I Find Out About Auditions?

Many auditions are listed in weekly trade newspapers, such as *Show Business* and *Backstage*, which are published in New York, and *Drama-Logue*, which is published in Hollywood. (The daily and weekly *Variety* gives information about the business aspect of the entertainment industry; it should not be considered a "casting" newspaper, despite the fact that a few casting notices appear in its pages.) These papers list every conceivable audition—Broadway, television, film, Las Vegas shows, modern dance, industrials, showcases, dinner theaters, children's theater—and are seen on newsstands in both Los Angeles and New York. If you are an aspiring performing artist in New York City, the usual ritual is to march to the local newsstand in the morning to pick up the "trades," then to sit down and commence the grueling task of circling prospective auditions, and finally to spend the day auditioning. Dance auditions are also advertised in flyers posted in dance schools, conservatories, colleges, and universities.

Most choreographers recommend that dancers do not over-'book themselves with too many audition appointments in one day. One audition alone can last most of a day, if you survive the process of elimination. If you find that you have overbooked, be sure to telephone and reschedule your other auditions.

There are also auditions that are not advertised. It is not uncommon for a choreographer to invite dancers to a private audition. Agents may also arrange private auditions for their clients.

What Is the Choreographer Looking For?

It is very difficult to be specific about what a choreographer looks for in a theatrical dancer; much depends on the production's book and the choreographer's own style and preference. Sometimes, it is not how talented or well trained the dancer is

"I am always looking for a well-centered human being. I used to concentrate on talent and technique, but today I look for much more: I look for the whole person. I draw my circle of those I am interested in and choose from the circle. I am very careful about the purity of the person. I like my people to be 360 degrees in scope. I believe that there is a tendency for auditionees to leave part of themselves in the wings when they step on stage. That is why I like to talk to my people before their audition, and ask them to tell me their favorite 'onstage performance.' This gives me some insight that I normally would not have during the audition. For each show, I have different things I am looking for: talent, type, voice, body, poise, concentration, depth, inner light . . . I want a lot!"
—Tommy Tune

"I look for the attitude of the dancer after the combination is completed. I am not impressed by those who apologize for their mistakes. I note those persons who attempt as well as achieve the correction I have given. If I know that they have tried to do what I want, that makes an important impression on me. Because of the time element, especially in television work, my dancers have to be 'quick studies.'"
—Tony Stevens

"The first thing I look for in an audition is the dancer's timing, sense of rhythm, musicality, and elements beyond training. Next, I look for technique founded in ballet. Everything else is secondary if they can learn quickly."
—Lee Theodore

"I should be considered odd in my type of casting. I look for people with great eyes. The audience is constantly looking for the truth, which is part of the book [script]. By having the truth, the dancer is using the tools to lift up the star [of the show]. It is essential. One can be very acrobatic, but more than that is wanted. The audience is not looking for technique but truth and that reading comes from the eyes. After looking for that element in the audition, I secondly watch for a person's rhythm or sense of musicianship."
—Geoffrey Holder

that really counts: "type casting" is common for shows that require particular physical types. Decisions made by the artistic staff and producers are also usual in the auditioning process. For an insight into what some choreographers look for, I asked Tommy Tune, Tony Stevens, Lee Theodore, and Geoffrey Holder for their ideas.

BROADWAY

What Will I Be Expected To Do?

While the approach to auditioning varies with each choreographer, there are certain basic requirements for which every prospective dancer should be prepared before attending an audition.

Because the Broadway dancer today has to sing as well as dance, you should always be ready to sing an up-tempo song and a ballad for a show audition. The auditioner will usually request just one song, but you should be prepared with another if he wants to hear more. I suggest that you sing your best up-tempo song first to show the quality of your voice and your vocal range. When the audition is a large "cattle call,"* do not be discouraged if the auditioner cuts you off after sixteen bars. He can usually get a good idea of what you can produce even with that short amount of vocalizing. The singing part of your audition might occur at the beginning or close of the audition, depending on the preference of the auditioner.

During the dance portion of the audition, most choreographers have an assistant to teach the dance combination or to aid them in the progress of the audition. Often, the choreographer will set the combination himself in order to emphasize certain ideas that he wants projected by the dancers. You may also be requested to perform several dance combinations in varying dance forms.

---

*"Cattle call" describes a large open audition for, usually, a limited number of contract openings. The group of dancers is said to be "herded in for the slaughter" by the auditioner.

Time is essential to the choreographer. He not only has limited hours during the audition process, but short rehearsal periods require him to cast "quick studies."* Combinations are shown only a few times, so pick up the feet first and add the other elements later. If you are a globular learner, one who perceives the total concept at once, you are fortunate. If you are a fragmentary learner, one who retains a combination bit by bit, focus on memorizing the steps first and the arms second. However you learn it do not forget to execute the combination at performance level each time. And smile! Even certain mistakes can be covered with a smile.

In a large cattle-call audition, you will be required to perform in small groups. Under grueling circumstances, you will perform the combination with the same group continually as the choreographer eliminates dancers. You may be dismissed or "type-casted" out immediately, or you may have a full day with the choreographer, going over many dance combinations, singing, and occasionally giving a "dry" reading† of the script or even a personal interview. If you survive the first audition, do not expect a contract offer that day. There are always callbacks, which involve more intensive work and more combinations to learn, or are devoted to pairing dancers for partnering purposes or for height evaluations. Days, weeks, and even months are taken to cast a show. Lee Theodore informed me that it took almost a year to complete the original cast of *West Side Story*. Be patient and do not get discouraged. Realize that among the many decisions to be made, few have to do with how well you auditioned.

Bob Fosse's *Dancin'* Auditions

In all my interviews, the most favorable responses were given to Bob Fosse's *Dancin'* auditions. Several dancers contributed the following statements about Mr. Fosse's approach.

*Performers who learn quickly.
†"Dry" reading is performing from a script with which the auditionee is totally unfamiliar.

WAYNE CILENTO

Unfortunately, Wayne Cilento's first audition with Bob Fosse was an unsuccessful attempt.

I went to his *Chicago* audition, which included performing the infamous "Tea for Two" number.* At the cattle-call dance audition and the singing audition, I was type-casted out.

After *A Chorus Line,* I was on the road with *The Act* for six months, so I missed Bob's *Dancin'* Equity call. Graciela Daniele, choreographer for the New York production of *Pirates of Penzance* and, most recently, the revival on Broadway of *Zorba,* was kind enough to suggest to Bob that he try to give me an audition. Because of that, I was invited to a private audition. It turned out to be very informal; the only other people present were Ann Reinking and the accompanist. We were one on one. Bob danced with me and taught the "Tea for Two" combination and another combination of steps from the show. I then sang for him. I especially remember singing quite well because I was so relaxed with him throughout the audition. At the end, he informed me that the casting had been completed but he would let me know if things changed. [Bob Fosse then went to preview performances of *The Act* to watch Wayne Cilento perform.] It was funny, for on opening night of *The Act* I knew I was cast in *Dancin'.*

Surprisingly, neither Barbara Hanks nor Tommy Peel, who have been cast in numerous shows, were cast in *Dancin',* yet Bob Fosse and Gwen Verdon still made it their most memorable audition.

---

*This is a standard Fosse combination that is given at many of his auditions. It combines ballet, with its jumps and turns, and jazz, in feeling and rhythmical patterns that are typical of his style. It is an excellent combination to show off the abilities of a dancer.

WAYNE CILENTO

BARBARA HANKS

I remember that I could not make the women's call for *Dancin'*, so I went to the men's Equity call and danced the much talked about "Tea for Two" number and another lyric jazz combination. I had to leave the audition to film a commercial, but Bob Fosse was kind enough to invite me back to a private audition with five other dancers the following week. Once again, I went through "Tea for Two," the lyrical jazz combination, and a rock jazz combination. After that, he cut two girls and proceeded to give the remaining three of us a tap combination with hand rhythms. Following that evaluation, he put some music on and we were asked to improvize. Last, but not least, we all sang. After completing the audition, Bob Fosse said he would telephone us about casting. What impressed me most was that he actually did take the time to telephone everyone, whether or not they made it! [Besides being impressed with his concern, Miss Hanks recognized that his audition was an excellent one to show strengths and weaknesses.] Auditions are so distressing because the dancers' relationship to the choreographer is so vulnerable. I guess that is why there are so many neurotic people in this business. There are not many who get a break. The pressure is unbearable, and you really have to know who you are spiritually, physically, and mentally. You must show that you have something special, and Mr. Fosse has the ability to let you do just that in his auditions.

TOMMY PEEL

The *Dancin'* audition given by Gwen Verdon in Los Angeles was my most memorable. Miss Verdon was so friendly and relaxed that she made everyone else feel at ease. Being a dancer herself, she could relate to everyone's problems in an audition. She also took the time to explain the moves in the combination, which were taken from the show itself. Warmups were not given in this audition, which is common in most show auditions that I have attended. Miss Verdon

BARBARA HANKS

TOMMY PEEL

taught Bob Fosse's "Tea for Two" combination, which identifies the real dancers and helps to weed out the others.

This Equity cattle call started with the dance audition and culminated in the elimination of all but ten dancers. I went into a singing audition after the dance audition, followed by a cold reading from the script. At the end of the audition, Gwen Verdon took four of the men's photographs and resumes back to New York for Mr. Fosse's evaluations. I was one of those four dancers under consideration, but unfortunately I did not get the job.

Both Barbara Hanks and Tommy Peel listed the *Dancin'* auditions as their most memorable.

CHARLES WARD

Charles Ward heard about the *Dancin'* auditions in New York from his agent. He had been out of American Ballet Theatre for some time and received, at the same time, an offer from Rudolph Nureyev to perform the role of Romeo in the Festival Ballet's production of *Romeo and Juliet*.

I accepted the offer with reservations, but after thinking about it I realized that I would be going back to a lifestyle which I had just discontinued with American Ballet Theatre. It was important for me to make the departure, to meet new people and have new contacts.

When I went to the *Dancin'* auditions, about twenty of the seventy-five dancers there I knew. I could feel people talking about me, despite the fact that I really did not expect to be recognized in the crowd, being so new to Broadway auditioning. [During the audition, Mr. Ward explained that he kept wondering when he was going to be eliminated, since Bob Fosse kept cutting people that looked like him.] After completing the audition, which included the "Tea for Two" combination, there were only a handful of us left. For me, there were two more auditions that I had to attend before being cast in this show. [Mr. Ward explained that the first audition was purely dance; the second, a singing audition mixed with conversation on his personal background; and the third, a singing audition with selections chosen by the musical director. Then, Mr. Fosse sat down with him and suggested that he was almost sure to be cast; which happened two weeks later.]

Bob Fosse's audition was the most memorable because of my being purely impressed with the body of his work. He is a very intense man; it is hard to put a finger on his charisma. He demands attention and is a brilliant director. He is very comfortable to be around, he respects his dancers a lot, and he takes the time to tell them what he wants from them.

When Do I Open On Broadway?

Many dancers have the misconception that shows instantly open on Broadway after the allotted rehearsal period is completed. In reality, a great deal of time passes before a show's Broadway debut. After the lengthy process of casting, which can go on for six months or longer, dates are set for rehearsals, which usually last five to six weeks. Following that, the company leaves on tour for several weeks or months, during which time any flaws are ironed out.

Sugar Babies is a typical example of what many shows undergo before opening in New York. When Barbara Hanks started touring with Sugar Babies, she found herself in San Francisco for a seven-week engagement of the show. She says that Sugar Babies changed drastically during its five months on tour. The cast would rehearse a new number or skits during the day and perform the old choreography and blocking* that night. Sometimes, the stars of the show would try out a new song in performance. The cast was constantly switching gears because of the many rewrites, but this process was the only way to tighten the show before producing it on Broadway.

Philadelphia was the last touring stop, at which time they were in the final smoothing out stages. When they arrived on Broadway, the cast had a few days to rehearse in the theater with a stage crew that had traveled with the show. After one week of preview performances, the show finally opened on Broadway.

INDUSTRIALS

Another outlet for dancers that is often overlooked is industrial shows. Industrials are mini-musicals, produced by large corporations and companies to advertise one or more products. A goodly number of car-and-truck industrials often incorporate special technical effects that can range from laser beams and smoke illusions to the appearance of dancing on the product itself. They pay well and often have top stars, an abundance of male and female dancers, a large production budget, and big dance numbers.

Industrials are usually publicized in the trade papers with other auditions, except smaller ones, which are publicized by an agent. Once you have performed in an industrial, it is much easier to get into another one if you are liked by the employers. Auditions are similar to those for Broadway shows, with an added element: dancers are often requested to talk while dancing to advertise the product.

*Pattern of movement around the stage.

TELEVISION AND FILM

Auditions for television and film are most often private. "The television dancer, unfortunately, is a small commodity in Los Angeles," says Tony Stevens, "and I can name just on my two hands the dancers who are regularly used. In Los Angeles, the casting is very selective and usually a dancer is called to do television work. Many times, a choreographer will have as many as twelve specials in a year. The casting is done through closed auditions because the choreographer not only does not have time for extensive auditions, but he knows who is good and on whom he can depend."

Tommy Peel, who can be listed as one of those fortunate television/club dancers, informed me that many of his television auditions were private or by invitation from the choreographer. He remembers his audition for *The Donny and Marie Show*. He initially found out about it by word of mouth from a fellow dancer. The audition was atypical because the choreographer observed him in a Las Vegas performance, then went backstage and paced him through a tap combination. That combination led to Mr. Peel's employment for the television series.

Both Tommy Peel and Tony Stevens mention that dancers often hear about television auditions by word of mouth or in the dance classes taught by popular Los Angeles instructors, who are often the choreographers for television shows. Dancers try to study with them in the hope of being invited to an audition. This is also true for films. Breaking into this type of work requires perseverence. As Tony Stevens succinctly puts it, "If you do not love it, do not do it."

What Must I Be Able To Do?

Those interested in auditioning for television or film must understand what is involved. Tony Stevens explained an interesting difference between television and film: "In television, you are working in a medium that deals with closeups to create the energy. As you see the full body, you see less and less of the energy because the image is smaller. Even though video cuts and angles help to present excitement, you can see how important a dancer's projection and body energy are in this medium." In my conversations with Mr. Stevens, I felt the frustration that he constantly faces when choreographing for television. "There are incredible demands placed on the choreographer to do the biggest and splashiest production with the least amount of time spent." In this situation, the dancer has to be not only a well-rounded performer, who can pick up routines quickly, but one who is in control during the most hectic times. For example, Mr. Stevens explained that costumes are often not ready until shooting, yet the first rehearsal in costume is usually the first video take of the number. There is only one blocking rehearsal, and a two-hour time period is standard for blocking and taping the number. Disorientation and spotting* problems—due to lights, cameras, equipment, and crews in motion— have to be overcome by the dancers. No excuses are accepted.

From a dancer's viewpoint, Tommy Peel explains, "A dancer will often have to psych himself for a television shooting since there are usually no audience responses. Although some shows are performed in front of a live studio audience, certain 'live' shows, like *The Donny and Marie Show,* tape certain skits and dances without one." I asked Tommy Peel about the time taken to record skits and dances on camera. He explained that there are occasions when the dancers have to stop and retake a certain section if the staff in the booth is not satisfied with the first take, but the first shooting is usually the one seen on television. When there are retakes, the dancer is confronted with the need to maintain spontaneity throughout. Patience is not only an asset, but a *must,* for the television dancer. "Occasionally, we would have a retake with the live studio audience," Mr. Peel continued. "Believe me, it is much more exhilarating when you perform in front of an audience, for you can really feed off their responses."

In comparing the time element for television and film, Geoffrey Holder has some observations. Having performed both on television and in films, Mr. Holder feels that a major

---

*Focusing while turning.

drawback in movie filming is the incredible amount of time spent sitting around waiting for the shooting of a dance number because of the many camera angles that have to be set up for each dance segment. He says that dancers in filmmaking not only have to be patient, but also aware that they will have to warm up repeatedly before one shooting is completed.

Despite the many hours of sitting around, the filming of movies offers quite a different element of excitement from television for the dancer and choreographer. The physical space allotted for filming permits much more creativity. In television, you are constantly working with cameras in the way; in movies, dancers have all the room necessary. There is also much more time assigned to the filming process because the lighting and setup time for each shooting is crucial to successful completion of the film. At times, there may be four cameras filming at once from one viewpoint, followed by a cut, so that cameras can be set for a closeup of the same scene.

The possibility of creating a sense of unity without being on the set is also a remarkable innovation in filmmaking—dancers might perform for eight counts on the lot, then suddenly reappear on a skyscraper for another eight counts. Tony Stevens choreographed several segments in the film version of *The Best Little Whorehouse in Texas* which employed a number of different locations in one dance number. I asked him how he had managed to create choreography in such a way. "I have always been involved with films, even when I was younger. I grew up seeing movies about twice a week. Through so much observation of film techniques, I have been able to develop my own concepts in choreographing for film. Dancing on a building and then having the dancers disappear and reappear in the theater is so exciting because you are constantly given the opportunity to combine fantasy and reality." Unlike television, in which the medium soaks up the energy of the dancer, Tony Stevens finds that films present a clearer sense of totality in movement energy.

What is also intriguing in Tony Steven's choreographic approach to the film, *The Best Little Whorehouse in Texas,* is that in

New York he employed a hand-picked skeleton crew of dancers on whom he set the choreography before actual production on the film started in Los Angeles. Barbara Hanks, one of the New York dancers selected for this crew, explained that, due to the time element, Mr. Stevens could not waste any precious moments with the choreographic process during the actual filming. All his choreographic material had to be ready to set on the film's dancers and stars.

An Audition With Tony Stevens

If there are strong or specific types needed, Tony Stevens "types out" the auditionees immediately, then requests those remaining to change into their dance clothes.

TONY STEVENS

If there is not a "type," I usually explain the style and what the combination is to do for me. For instance, if I were to do a jeans commercial, I may have a hoedown stylistic idea in mind. Whatever dance combination I present, I take a long time to teach it and hate being rushed by dancers who ask, "When are we going to perform the combination?" I let everybody feel like they know it well since there is a great deal of fear that builds up in the dancer when he thinks he does not know the combination. I change lines often, and find that adding humor by joking around with the auditionees or assistant helps eliminate a lot of nervous energy.

If I have seventy-five dancers, I will start in groups of twenty-five, so that they can feel the full extension of their movement. When making close observations, I only take six at a time because I really can not observe more than that. After watching the groups of six, I give personal notes and corrections. I also space the dancers three-and-three to see how aware they are of keeping their own spacing while dancing with other people. This is important; a dance chorus has to fit into given slots in the design of the choreography. I give specific notes, like clean arms and body placement, and then I run through the dancers in sixes again. I separate those I really like into an A list, those I have doubts about executing my style into a B list, and place those that are on their way out into a C list.

Depending on time, I usually have them line up to see how many dancers I have. Then, I check over the openings available. At callbacks, I pick out the favorites I want to see and tell them to relearn the combination from the previous day and be prepared to sing and read. I hardly ever show another combination at the callbacks, and make a point of giving performing notes before they dance the combination. Notes might include such images as drop, collapse, stretch, smile, seduce me. They go through it as a whole, then I break them down in groups.

I usually use an assistant in auditions, so that technical questions can be worked out with him. I do not like to be hassled with a lot of questions during auditions, so I let the assistant handle that for me. Usually, after conferring endlessly with the director, the decisions are made for casting. Dancers must realize that it is just as hard for us as it is for them to go through the decision-making process.

LAS VEGAS SHOWS

The shows produced in the major entertainment centers of Nevada are usually spectaculars—big, lavish, meant to convey beauty and fantasy—staged in large showrooms. They also pay high salaries (a benefit of this type of career) which draws dancers ranging from professional ballet dancers to ex-hoofers. Adrian Le Peltier, experienced show manager and dance captain,* says that "The only problem with such big shows is that all too often the dancers cry 'boredom' after a certain amount of time. You have the same routine with no real semblance of change."

---

*Dance captains are the liaison between the management staff and the dancers. Their duties vary with each show and the number of dancers they represent, but regularly they are responsible for rehearsing the dancers, holding auditions when requested, and covering for any problems that might arise due to sickness or injury. They also ensure that the dancers' conduct and the performance of the choreography is correct at all times.

*From hoedown dances...to a touch of sophistication...*Raw Satin *represents the versatility of today's dancers. This popular performing group, which is based in Los Angeles, frequently brings their club show to Las Vegas. (Tommy Peel, Victor Heineman, Tony White, Wade Collings, Richard Montoya, Cortlandt Jones, Rick Rozzini).*

He suggests that dancers find out what "type" is wanted for a particular Las Vegas show before auditioning. A principal requirement, given the size of the shows, is height, especially the men. Even a six-foot male dancer can appear small on stage dancing next to a showgirl wearing heels and a four-foot headdress. Roughly, men should be 6' and up, showgirls and nudes (showgirls who perform topless) 5'7" and up, and ponies (short topless dancers) 5'6" and up. Attractiveness is also of prime importance. Frequently, a choreographer will hire a dancer lacking in certain skills and spend time training that dancer, if he or she has the right look for the show.

Nevertheless, the Las Vegas show dancer should be proficient in a variety of musical comedy dance forms. Mr. Le Peltier explains that classical ballet and jazz, in particular, are important. "If a person has occasion to learn acrobatics, tumbling, folk, or tap, he should definitely pursue it because show requirements are constantly changing." He also mentions that adagio (which, in show dancing, consists of partnering with emphasis on lifts) training is a great help. A male-female adagio partnership is a specialty that pays more and can be developed even during the run of a show. If a pair of company dancers are interested in an adagio team position, they get permission from their dance captains and/or company manager to rehearse together, usually between shows or during assigned rehearsal periods. When they feel fully prepared, an informal audition for the dance captains and/or company manager is held, often between shows. If the dancers are successful, they are given an understudy position, which will allow them to perform when the other adagio team(s) is sick, injured, or on leave of absence. With time, they may work themselves into a permanent adagio team position.

How Do I Get To Audition?

Las Vegas show dancers are often the same ones seen on television as backup dancers for such well-known performers as Ann-Margret or Juliet Prowse. However, this should not prevent any dancer from seeking an audition, since a second type of Las Vegas dancer performs on a six-month or one-year contract.

A major advantage of show auditions is that you can telephone for one at any time of the year. Despite the fact that contracts are given every six months at open cattle calls, the dance captains will give auditions either before or after their nightly show. The dance captains are friendly, but businesslike, in their approach and are only too willing to audition anyone who feels that he can qualify for the job. If you are successful but there is no present job opening, the dance captain will file your audition card for future reference.

Aside from your ability to perform well in the audition, there are certain recommendations to keep in mind. Although the shows themselves are very glamourous, you should not overdo that aspect for the audition. Adrian Le Peltier feels that dancers should not wear dancewear that is gimmicky or trendy: "I personally do not like to see jewelry or leg warmers worn," he says. The prohibition against jewelry should be taken seriously; it is a danger and a distraction.

Private Versus Open Call

To give you an example of Las Vegas dance auditions, I would like to recall for you the chain of events which led to my employment at the M.G.M. Grand Hotel in Reno, Nevada.

> After teaching college for seven years, I got what you might call the seven-year itch to perform full time. I primarily wanted to prove to myself that I could still make it through the auditioning process and maintain a full-time performing job at the age of thirty.
>
> Before I left for Las Vegas and Reno to audition, I wrote to ask my friend, Tommy Peel, about the qualifications. He answered that I should not have any problems because I qualified in the three major areas: height, attractiveness, and dance ability. Once I knew that, I wrote to the dance captains of various major shows in Las Vegas and Reno to find out about audition dates. (Because of the six-month contract schedule, most open cattle-call auditions occur

around the middle of February and August.) I received a response, which included information on the cattle-call auditions, from each dance captain. Even if I were unable to attend the open calls, the captains were kind enough to offer a private audition before or after their shows.

At the end of a summer-stock season, I went to Reno in mid-August and telephoned Adrian Le Peltier backstage at the M.G.M. Grand Hotel in Reno for an audition. He kindly responded by scheduling a time for the next day before his first show. The audition was given on stage, and was quite distracting at that particular hour because of the chatter of the audience on the other side of the main drape and the constant crossovers made by the technical crew and dancers preparing for the first show. However, I focused on Adrian as he paced me through two combinations from the show. The first, a tricky top-hat number with a cane in one hand while the other mimed the top-hat movements, was a real challenge. The second combination was a jazz dance, which just happened to have pirouettes to the left. (If you are not technically strong on both sides, it could be a drawback in an audition like this.) I was particularly impressed with Mr. Le Peltier's patience, as an auditioner, in giving me plenty of time to feel comfortable with the combinations.

After the audition, he filled out an information card for his own file and informed me that he would know in another week if there was an opening in the Reno show. He not only gave me positive criticism, uncommon in most auditioners, but was kind enough to arrange a recommendation by telephone when I told him my intent to audition for the M.G.M. Grand Hotel in Las Vegas.

The M.G.M. audition I attended in Las Vegas was one of the semiannual open cattle calls held in the main showroom. As I entered the massive theater, I was met by a dance captain who asked me to fill out an information card. (I recommend that all dancers present a resume and photograph with any such data card they are requested to complete. It adds a touch of professionalism, which can help to impress the auditioner.)

I will always remember my first impressions of the showroom, its beauty and the spectacular size of the stage. I was also somewhat frightened as I warmed up along with many other male dancers stationed around white table-clothed tables and red velvet chairs used as ballet barres.

There were approximately forty women on stage completing the last part of their audition while the male dancers warmed up. As I observed the women's audition, I realized that the showgirl of today has changed tremendously. The statuesque beauties who used to walk and pose in feathered costumes are now required to dance—and dance well. So must the corps of topless dancers. At the end of the general dance audition, those women who were interested in becoming nude dancers were asked to line up on stage for physique evaluations. For the most part, these evaluations were handled without disrobing, although a dancer might be asked to lower her leotard (at times, this is done in the privacy of another room at the request of the dancer). Nudes, of course, make more money. For many female dancers, it is just a matter of personal preference.

The men's audition immediately followed the women's evaluations. It started with a jazz combination taught by the boy's dance captain. (The sequence in the men's audition is similar to that in the women's, which was given by the girl's dance captain.) All sixty male auditionees learned the combination together and ran through it a few times in groups. We were then asked to cross the stage, one at a time, executing a ballet combination of turns. If the dancer reached center stage before Donn Arden, the producer-director of both the Las Vegas and Reno shows, called out "thank you" as a means of dismissal, the dancer continued to the other side to join the survivors. From that small ballet combination alone the numbers were reduced from sixty to twenty. We twenty were taught another combination that used modern dance movements. I was surprised that this type of combination was being thrown at show dancers; it is not typical in these auditions. As soon as Mr. Arden saw that the majority of dancers were struggling with the combination, he asked the dance captain to proceed with another part of the audition.

Since Mr. Arden wanted to observe individual performances by the auditionees, the dance captain requested each of us to create and perform a thirty-two count combination in any dance form we wished. We had five minutes to work on developing this small composition. I was quite surprised with the many variations that were performed. Most were jazz-oriented, but there were a few ballet combinations and even one modern combination. Following the solo performances, Donn Arden made a few more eliminations.

The next part of the audition, the physique evaluation, is typical of Las Vegas show auditions, but took me by surprise. We were asked to strip down to our dance belts in the wings, then stand in line on stage. The feeling of being exposed under heavy stage lighting, on a bare stage, in front of auditioners and women auditionees alike, was a distressing experience. I prayed it would end quickly. The purpose of this type of evaluation is to see what the physique will look like in the g-string costumes that are common to Las Vegas shows. (A flabby stomach does not have a chance in this type of an evaluation. Rectify your weight problems before auditioning.)

After we scrambled to put our clothes back on, we were once again asked to stand in line for further evaluations. Mr. Arden went down the line asking each dancer a few personal questions in order to gauge his personality and the validity of the information on his audition card or resume. He also dismissed a few primarily because of height and weight problems. There were five of us left after the short interview. Mr. Arden informed us that he could not make any decisions just then, and requested us to return the following day. To say the least, the news was exasperating, but the surprise was still to come.

When I arrived the next day, I noticed that the entire male chorus from the M.G.M. show was warming up with the four other dancers who were called back. Not only did the five of us dance through another audition similar to the one we had experienced the previous day, but we soon found out that we were competing against the company members, who were auditioning for new contracts. After completing familiar jazz combinations, our best thirty-two-count composition, and the physique evaluation, we were once again directed to line up at the front of the stage. This time, Mr.

Arden announced that we were all to be offered a thirteen-month contract. The five of us, who were the "new boys," never knew until that day that there were five openings. I am sure the callback was scheduled primarily to see how well we looked among the other company members.

That should have been the happy ending to my Las Vegas auditions, but there was more. Once the contracts were offered, I inquired about a possible opening in the Reno show. Of course, the other four new dancers thought I was crazy, but I had reasons for asking. First of all, I had graduated from Reno High School and knew the area and people, which made it much more appealing to me than Las Vegas. Secondly, I had observed both the Reno and Las Vegas shows before auditioning and knew the dancing in Reno would be more challenging. Donn Arden was very accommodating. He suggested that I check in Reno a week later, when he would know exactly how many openings there would be in the show there, *Hello Hollywood Hello*.

When I returned to Reno a week later, I telephoned Adrian Le Peltier immediately to explain the situation. He gave me an audition time for the following day, although I still did not know exactly what was going to happen. I met Mr. Le Peltier at the stage door, where I was introduced to another dancer who was also auditioning. In a backstage corner, Mr. Le Peltier paced us through the top-hat and jazz numbers until we were comfortable with the movement and clean in our execution. Meanwhile, we could hear singers auditioning on stage for what I thought was just a private audition. After we had learned both combinations, Mr. Le Peltier announced that we were not just auditioning for him; we were to go on stage and perform for Donn Arden and the Reno company manager. I sighed with relief when Mr. Le Peltier reassured us that he would perform the lengthy combinations with us.

As I walked on stage, I was immediately blinded by the stage lights, which made it virtually impossible to spot, let alone determine who was evaluating us in the showroom. It was not until later that I discovered that, in addition to Donn Arden and the company manager, the singers from the show who had just finished reauditioning were observing. We performed the entire top-hat combination with music and, to our surprise, received applause from the singers. Donn Arden called from the house that he was pleased with our performance of the number, especially as we had had such a short time to practice. I proceeded to go through my third physique evaluation, and then awaited the final decision. After conferring with Mr. Arden, Mr. Le Peltier came back on stage and informed us that there was only one opening in the Reno show. The producer had decided to offer the contract to me.

5

BALLET AUDITIONS

★★

The qualifications for entry into a professional ballet company are discussed in this chapter by the following dancers, choreographers, and directors.

DANIEL DUELL
Principal dancer in the New York City Ballet.

RICHARD ENGLUND
Choreographer and director of American Ballet Theatre II, the second company of American Ballet Theatre.

ROBERT JOFFREY
Choreographer, teacher, and founder and director of the City Center Joffrey Ballet.

DONALD MAHLER
Director of the Metropolitan Opera Ballet Ensemble.

PATRICIA ROZOW
Principal dancer in the Cincinnati Ballet Company.

DENNIS WAYNE
Former dancer with the Norman Walker, Harkness, Joffrey, and American Ballet Theatre companies; founder and director of Dancers.

REBECCA WRIGHT

Former principal dancer in the City Center Joffrey Ballet and soloist in American Ballet Theatre.

TRAINING

When contemplating a professional ballet career, take its requirements into consideration. Not only is sound ballet technique needed, but also character dance. Part of many classical ballets, this form is frequently taught in ballet schools. Modern dance, which used to be absent from ballet schools, is now another valuable part of the curriculum. Today's ballet repertoires have both modern and jazz choreography, so a good

The Metropolitan Opera Ballet in Cindrella *with Martha Purl and Virgil Pearson-Smith.*

Stephen Driscoll

Dennis Wayne's Dancers company.

background in these areas is vital to the dancer. Mime is also an important part of the ballet dancer's training and is often offered as a special course or as an extension of a ballet technique class.

The Individual

Females. Training must start early enough to acquire the necessary skills for performing well on pointe. The average age for a young ballerina to be accepted into a company is seventeen or eighteen. Companies will usually consider dancers over the age of twenty only if they have had previous performance experience in another company. Weight and height must be carefully considered before auditioning for a ballet company. A slender, toned physique is a necessity. The tall ballerina is still in great demand in major ballet companies. This is not to say that shorter female dancers are not used, but many directors prefer the elongated classical line that a taller ballerina can convey in performing the repertoire.

Male. The potential male ballet dancer should begin to investigate dance at a young age, as soon as he expresses interest in the art. However, because of the negative stereotype that still attaches to men in ballet, many male dancers tend to begin training in later years. Men *may* start training as late as their college years and still achieve the necessary skill to audition for a ballet company because they do not have to spend years building the strength needed for performance on pointe. Of course, in order to excel as a male ballet dancer, you must have physical strength, good flexibility, the ability to comprehend and execute movement skills proficiently, and control of the physique, which are often facilitated by the increase in strength associated with post-adolescence. The young male dancer should not be discouraged from attempting a career in ballet if he has not started to work daily in his early teens because the potential for success comes from discipline and dedication at any time.

The only real disadvantage for the male dancer auditioning for a company is being too short for adagio, or partner work, a major concern for most companies. An acceptable height range is 5'8" to 5'11"; if you are shorter, you must be more talented. Since the availability of talented male ballet dancers is still limited, a company may make an exception even if there is a height problem.

Both. Patricia Rozow states that girls should take beginning ballet classes twice a week at age eight and three times a week at age ten. She also suggests that by age twelve or thirteen, young dancers should be exposed to some modern, jazz, and even tap dance. She also points out that having a good background in music and being able to play an instrument will help the development of a ballet dancer. Daniel Duell adds that, for optimum training, a regimen of daily classes should be taken by age twelve or thirteen for girls and thirteen or fourteen for boys.

Rebecca Wright feels that dancers between ages sixteen and eighteen should develop a strong sense of themselves as a person. "One must be physically and emotionally prepared to deal with either being accepted or rejected from the audition," she says. She also recommends that a dancer should know anatomy and choreography, and be aware of the internal organization of the company: the interpersonal relations between directors, choreographers, designers, and dancers. Further, "Some background in character dance is helpful, although the refinement of the form is usually achieved in the company."

In comparing notes, I though Daniel Duell gave one of the most significant statements about the training of the dancer of today: "A solid grounding in basic classical ballet technique is essential, as it forms the most complete point of departure for nearly all dance forms." This belief is shared by many artists and should be acknowledged by young dancers who are preparing for any kind of audition—ballet, Broadway, television, film, even Las Vegas shows.

When I inquired about specific body-type qualifications, Mr. Duell replied, "Generally, the dancer should have aesthetically appealing proportions, flexible joints, supple musculature to prevent injury, and well-arched or flexible feet, and the ability to 'turn out' is very important." Rebecca Wright adds, "The student should have rhythm, good coordination, intelligence, and a driving desire to perform." "I do not think anyone should be discouraged by the body requirements in ballet," says Patricia Rozow, "but they should be made aware of what an 'ideal' dancer's body should be. Knowing one's shortcomings will enable one to make the best of other assets. We must make the best of what we have."

The challenge for today's ballet dancer is to compete against a high level of technical proficiency. Not everyone rises to this level, but sincerity and projection in performance can often outweigh technical deficiencies. If you are not the ideal ballet dancer, you may have to work harder to achieve your goal. Have faith in yourself.

Schools

Major Companies.   Ballet companies often have their own schools in which they can train dancers from a very young age until they are ready to audition for the company. There is, therefore, an advantage to attending such schools. The School of American Ballet is the official school of the New York City Ballet Company; American Ballet Theatre also has its school in New York. Qualified students who audition for either of these schools may receive a scholarship if they prove their professional potential.

Regional Companies.   Regional ballet companies are seen all over the United States and play an important role in the dance world. These companies are usually semiprofessional and provide a performing outlet for numerous dancers who would not otherwise have a chance to perform in larger ballet companies. Many of these dancers are drawn from local ballet schools in the community. Regional ballet companies also have their own schools in which students who want to perform in the company are trained and prospective professionals are prepared for a major ballet company audition. I recommend that those students who desire a career in ballet start in a reputable regional ballet school, if they cannot afford to go to a major conservatory or ballet school.

The National Endowment for the Arts sometimes provides financial support for professional touring companies which are extensions of the mother company. This offers valuable experience to a young dancer just starting out. Regional ballet companies are one of the most valuable assets for the growth and development of ballet throughout the United States and for the education of dance audiences. Many dancers who do not want to go into big city companies enjoy performing with regional ballet companies. They are also a good testing ground for aspiring choreographers.

Randy Batista

Kathryn Dandois and Tim Heflin of the Gainesville (Florida) Civic Ballet.

AUDITIONS

The ballet audition differs from the show or musical theater audition because it takes the form of a class. All the dancers auditioning together take the class, which often follows the standard regimen.

Barre Warmup.   There should be a progression of warmup exercises consisting of a variety of basic to advanced combinations (e.g., *pliés, port de bras, tendus, dégagés, frappés, ronds de jambe, fondus, battements*).

Center Floor Work (Adagio).   Slow work without the barre to show the dancers' strength, flexibility, and poise. Emphasis is on changing directions with the body, head, and arms and on combinations which include slow *développés, arabesques,* and balances.

Allegro.   Combinations that show *ballon* as well as skills in fast footwork and dynamics, such as jumps, turns, and traveling movements. Occasionally, an allegro combination will be taken from the company's repertoire.

Men's Grand Allegro.   This is usually done while the women change into pointe shoes. It consists of *double tours* and *beats* that the male dancer is expected to perform with *ballon* and sharpness.

Pointe Work.   The female dancers will be expected to execute a variety of skills on pointe in adagio and allegro combinations. *Pirouettes, jetés, beats, chaînés,* and *bourrées* are common. Also, be prepared to do all movements on both sides, which shows quickness of response, versatility, and strength.

Partnering.   This is often a crucial part of a ballet audition. It requires balancing skill and the ability to lift or be lifted. Men should have strength and a good sense of timing. Women should be able to balance while being partnered, to execute a movement and convey the correct body line in a lift or during a balance, and should also have a sense of timing.

For the female dancer, partnering can be the most exas-

Kathryn Dandois and Tim Heflin in the   *Helene Roux and Dennis Wayne of Dancers.*
Black Swan Pas de Deux.

Partnering skills are needed for classical as well as contemporary choreography.

perating part of an audition. She is at the mercy of the male dancer to move her through a combination successfully. Since the proportion of female to male dancers is so unequal, many women do not have the opportunity to acquire extensive partnering experience in class. They find themselves in a very precarious situation when asked to partner with an unknown male dancer at an audition.

I can only suggest that you try to work for a sense of timing with your partner, so that you can do the movements and lifts with the least amount of strain. The proper timing will also help a male dancer who does not have a great deal of strength to lift successfully.

What the Auditioner Looks For

The artists who were kind enough to share their ideas, experiences, and approaches with me also pointed out the differences between ballet and other types of auditions as well as today's changing requirements for a ballet career.

Jack Mitchell

RICHARD ENGLUND

Richard Englund has formulated a seminar on auditioning that
he presents at regional ballet festivals. He reminisces about his
entry as a dancer into Ballet Theatre company, through
performance observation rather than an audition. He remembers day-long musical theater auditions—in which the "look"
was most important—spent executing first *port de bras* or being
shifted endlessly from group to group, an unsettling experience.
His variety of background has given him a flexible approach to
ballet auditioning.

> Generally, I am surprised by today's ballet dancers who are
> less interested in an overall view of dance than in technique.

A ballet dancer is capable of dealing with other forms, such as folk dancing, and training now is extensive enough to acquire proficiency in other forms, although some approaches, such as improvisation, are very difficult for the ballet-trained dancer. I am very sorry that we may be going back to the mechanization of ballet by demanding the perfect body over more interesting dancers.

I look for several different qualities. As a choreographer, I want a spark and a sense of performance that is theatrical. I look for a creative dancer, not in the sense of one who improvises well, but one who contributes to the dimensions of the choreography. As the director of a repertory company, my major concern is versatility.

Another thing I look for is age. At Ballet Theatre, we are working with very young dancers. In ballet, it is not unusual to see young women auditioning at the ages of thirteen and fourteen, and there are those performing in companies as young as fifteen and sixteen. Since men usually start later in life, they are somewhat older. I personally believe that directors should up the age requirement. For one thing, maturity is often required for particular roles. I often feel that we are abusing our young talent by disregarding their adolescent development. To remove a young dancer from his peers and put him to work with a company that is not in the same age group can be a detriment: he loses his identity in the specialized state of a ballet company. I am afraid that building a ballet audience with young dancers is not a help either. Many dancers turn against the art form with bitterness because age has prevented them from excelling or continuing in their career.

Before an audition, I always explain what I am looking for as a way of easing the minds of young dancers. For example, I might say that I need four female dancers over 5'6" and one 5'4" female dancer. Young dancers should prepare themselves for height requirements. If they are in the middle category, they are in safe territory, but if they are unusually short or tall they must be exceptional. An audition can be the most harrowing and honest experience. You must come to grips with yourself when auditioning, for it can be traumatic.

I particularly enjoy an audition that uses movement approaches. This allows me to see how dancers absorb the movement. Unfortunately, auditions usually require split-second reactions, and I have noticed that some of our more valuable dancers do not project well in that type of situation. Foreign dancers, particularly, have the problem because they are used to material that developed out of a set school syllabus, which they have studied for years.

I group dancers, which is typical for ballet auditions, but I make sure I mix the yes's and the no's together, not because I want to trick them, but in the hope of keeping them sane throughout the audition. When I direct an audition, I focus on loosening up the dancers, especially since the process is so traumatic in itself.

Today's ballet dancer may find himself auditioning three times before the company offers him a contract. After the first audition, a dancer may be asked to take company class. The callback is usually a means for the artistic staff to get together and observe the auditionee. In the audition, it is not unusual for the dancer to be asked to perform a *pas de deux* and part of a repertory work he has been taught. Each audition is handled differently according to what the company needs at the particular time. Because American Ballet Theatre II is a transition company, we have a more extensive audition to fill the numerous openings in the company each season.

As for contracts, we have been burned by full-year contracts because we deal with young and inexperienced dancers. We now provide contracts that cover several periods of time related to our performing weeks in the year. The most irritating situation is when a dancer does not accept the job once it is offered. Many directors have noted that this is a major problem. Auditionees should be considerate of the auditioners and provide good reasons for not accepting a contract. Otherwise, it is not only a bad policy, but may result in blackballing that dancer from future auditions.

Herbert Migdoll

ROBERT JOFFREY

First of all, a ballet dancer should be fully prepared before coming to New York to audition. It is a good idea to call or write in advance to see when auditions are going to be held. A letter or recommendation from a teacher with whom one has studied is helpful, but not essential.

I like to see well-groomed ballet dancers at an audition. [Women in pink tights, leotard, pointe shoes, and ballet slippers; neat hair; and simple makeup. Men in dark tights, white tee shirt, and neat footwear. No one should wear baggy apparel; it is important that the muscles and body be easily seen.]

The dancer should know exactly which company he wants to belong to artistically. He should admire its repertoire and want to dance in its ballets. Too often, dancers rush into the first audition available and later regret the audition experience or are disillusioned with the company they hurriedly joined.

REBECCA WRIGHT

Look at the company, observe its style and artistic sensibilities. After you have done that, and you think you have the proper image for that company, audition for it. Always go where you think you are going to be liked. Most companies have specific types; be prepared to be judged in that manner. The class audition is cut and dried: there is no direct communication except for the teacher conducting class.

[Tradition has developed "ranks" within a ballet company, from corps to soloist to principal.] Ranks are more prominent in some of today's ballet companies than in others. The procedure can be either devastating to a dancer's career or one of its greatest goals. The dancer who joins a ballet company must be prepared emotionally to accept this hierarchical system.

DENNIS WAYNE

Dancers is a small, highly professional group, performing the best possible choreography, so I value quality in creativity and performance. The dancers' intellectual growth is extremely important to me. They should have a good understanding of all the arts and a strong background in theatrical training, since it is so closely allied with dance. Because the company tours overseas, the dancers should learn lan-

REBECCA WRIGHT

DENNIS WAYNE

guages, be open to other cultures, and be adaptable in all situations. I want them to be curious. Harmonious relationships, through sharing, contribute to the ensemble work of the company.

A true artist should be able to perform all forms of dance. Dancers alienate themselves by categorizing themselves, and I, for one, am not interested in just ballet dancers, although dancers should acquire sound ballet training. In addition, considering the abundance of modern choreography being produced, modern dance is essential. It is important to choose instructors carefully. In order for a dancer to achieve full potential as a performer, he must respect and not fear his teacher. Too many teachers of today are not pushing their students hard enough. Students take what might be called "fun" classes in order to avoid those that are more demanding.

Today's ballet dancer should approach the audition keeping several objectives in mind:

Be open to anything and everything given in the audition, no matter if you are asked to walk or crawl across the floor.

Perform only what is requested. So often, dancers will try to impress me by doing five, rather than the two stipulated *pirouettes.* Follow instructions.

Take correction well and apply it. I think the best audition is watching a dancer four hours a day, six days a week, and observing how he takes correction, applies it, and grows.

Be totally involved and willing to take chances with new ideas.

Project a positive attitude about the audition. This art form is too hard and demanding to allow for anything but affirmative attitude.

Know something about the taste of the directors and what they like from their dancers.

Be prepared to verbalize your thoughts, without undue ego, about why you want to be in the company.

Male dancers should project a strong male image.

Besides the usual barre warmup, center adagio, and jump combinations, I find it useful to use a combination from the repertoire. I must know how auditionees handle various styles, since new pieces are frequently added to the repertoire by guest choreographers.

I enjoy the opportunity to audition and hire dancers who have been rejected by major American ballet companies because they lacked the perfect body or technique. Potential can be just as impressive, and these are the dancers that often become valued performers.

DONALD MAHLER

The Metropolitan Opera Ballet Ensemble serves double duty as both an in-house and a touring company. I look for dancers who have the qualities to perform in both situations.

My approach to auditioning is necessarily geared to the Metropolitan Opera house, with its awesome stage space, lavish sets and costumes, and enormous casts. The dancers must be able to project well and act. Personality is just as important as technique for opera ballets as well as the ballets in our touring repertoire. The perfect body type is not the principal requirement.

I feel that ballet training today often produces dancers who place too much emphasis on steps rather than movements that really lead to dancing. I look for movement aesthetics and the potential for projecting the needed style. Character dance regularly appears in opera ballets, so I give audition combinations that show the dancer's musicality or rhythm—stylized forms, such as waltz variations or even a court dance. This way, I can observe much more than just the technical proficiency a dancer shows. A dancer with physical limitations may be turned down, but consideration is given to those who have potential for development. I do prefer artistic maturity in the dancers, even though the ages may range from the teens to the thirties.

I recommend that dancers take stock of themselves well before an audition. For example, a female dancer with a weight problem, who is going to audition in a couple of months, should lose that extra weight and not try to hide it under a chiffon skirt. A positive and disciplined attitude is also important. A dancer can project individuality without pushiness. If I allow the dancers to perform the combinations several times, I do not want to see them push their way to the front continually.

Proper appearance is also vital. Many auditionees seem to lack knowledge of the proper dress for ballet auditions, which can reveal the dancer's attitude about the audition, the job, and the auditioner. Dirty, torn, or sloppy dancewear may turn up in the studio, but in an audition, they convey lack of respect to the auditioner.

Open auditions are held, but I have hired more dancers from company class audition. Usually, they have called ahead of time for permission to audition during class or have come recommended by one of the company members. [This "open-door" way of making a job application is useful and not unique to the Metropolitan. Take the initiative to write or telephone the company of your choice about this type of audition.] When I give an open-call audition, I do not dismiss anyone during the audition, but wait until the end to allow the really talented dancer time to shine.

Prospective company members are also given a personal interview before a contract is signed. It includes an explanation of the nature of the job, what to expect, and what not to expect. I also ask dancers what they expect from the job, which gives me insight into their goals as well as their attitude and personality.

What the Dancer Looks For

Daniel Duell and Patricia Rozow have provided a variety of comments on the benefits and drawbacks of a ballet career which I feel exemplify the ideals shared by many artists in the dance world.

DANIEL DUELL

The benefits and drawbacks are similar to most performing arts careers. Personal fulfillment, possible stardom, the satisfaction of intense physical and mental effort, and the simultaneous development of these are a few of the benefits. Drawbacks include injuries, possible unemployment, or frustration from unrealized goals. If one is happy dancing, the drawbacks are far less than the benefits.

PATRICIA ROZOW

The ability to bring beauty to people as well as the accomplishments of physical feats and the joy of movement are major rewards in ballet performing. Also, the discipline, which carries over into life, is a personal benefit. Since many companies tour, you can experience interesting cities and have your artistry seen by a variety of audiences who enjoy the art form.

The drawbacks are many. Injury is a constant worry, even fear of injury if you indulge in doing sports. A dancer's schedule often makes social life difficult. It is hard for a

Arthur Elgort

PATRICIA ROZOW   *DANIEL DUELL*

nondancer to understand what it takes to be a dancer. It is a strain on a marriage, especially when one is touring.

A professional ballet career is short-lived and full of aches and pains. To make the necessary sacrifice and to dedicate sufficient time to being a good dancer is a big choice. It takes perseverence, courage, and a strong sense of self. It is a world in which you hear about your faults, while words of praise are few and far between. But the pluses must outweigh the minuses because many dancers do "make it."

Sometimes, I wonder why I am in the profession, but most of the time it is a way of life I enjoy. It can be just a good rehearsal or a fantastic performance that makes the work worth it. When I see an audience enjoying a ballet, it confirms my belief that I have chosen the right profession.

6

MODERN DANCE AUDITIONS

★★★★★★★★★★★★★★★★★★★★★★★★★★★★★★★★★★★★★

The diversity of styles in modern dance opens up an approach to auditioning that is different from other dance forms, a fact that is reflected in the views of artists who were interviewed for this chapter.

ERICK HAWKINS

Former dancer with the American Ballet, Ballet Caravan, and the Martha Graham company. Founder, director, and choreographer of his own company, stressing works of flowing movement and the use of commissioned live music scores.

PHYLLIS LAMHUT

Former dancer with the Alwin Nikolais and Murray Louis dance companies. Founder, director, and choreographer of her own company, specializing in pure movement, dramatic, and humorous works.

MURRAY LOUIS

Long-time associate of Alwin Nikolais. Founder, director, and choreographer of his own company, presenting works of supple and subtle muscular control.

DAN WAGONER

Former dancer with the Martha Graham and Paul Taylor companies. Founder, director, and choreographer of his own company, with a repertoire that states his personal feelings and warm human concern.

When modern dance started developing as a movement opposed to the academic structure of classical ballet, it focused on a freer, more natural way of expression. Now, it is not only a highly respected form in the dance world, but its development and growth has carried its style and choreography into the repertoire of ballet companies.

Although ballet and modern dance evolved along parallel lines for many years, we now see crossover in these two forms of dance. Ballet schools are requiring modern dance in their curriculum and certain modern dance companies (Twyla Tharp's is one example) and schools require ballet training. Because of the diversity in modern styles, there has been a tremendous growth of modern dance throughout the United States as well as in New York City. This has enabled many more dancers to perform professionally.

TRAINING

One advantage of a modern dance career is that it is possible for training to start later than it must for classical ballet. There is such diversity in height and physical types in modern dance that the form is more appealing to those dancers who do not have the ideal ballet body. Also, the less arduous physical requirements, such as not having to dance on pointe, will often allow the dancer to enjoy a longer performing career.

Nevertheless, the technical demands of modern dance have become as intricate as ballet. Today, a dancer can acquire solid technical training in the approaches of a diversity of modern schools. Since most modern dance companies have certain techniques that separate them from others, it may be necessary to make a choice among them. It is always wise to get as much insight as possible into the company in which you are interested by observing performances, initially taking a master class from a

José Limón Dance Company

Fernando Suarez

company member or the artistic director, and, eventually, attending regular classes.

Many companies offer classes at varying levels in their schools, while others provide company classes primarily for their dancers. By studying with the company, you will come to learn and understand its technique and to decide how serious your commitment is to this company. A company is much more willing to hire someone who has been exposed to its training and has committed himself to working toward an opening in that company.

To avoid later disillusionment, there are some other things to look for:

Do the company members get along with one another?

Do you think you will fit stylistically into the company?

Is the technique right for you?

What is the artistic staff like?

How are the rehearsals handled?

If you really believe that this is the company to which you want to belong, make it known to the director and work hard to achieve its style.

AUDITIONS

Modern dance auditions may occur almost anywhere across the country and are advertised in the local newspaper. In major cities, announcements appear in trade papers or on flyers that are posted in dance studios.

Most modern auditions are given as a class and will include warmups, combinations, perhaps locomotor movements across the floor, and even improvisation. There are many different approaches used in modern dance auditions, but remember that the auditioner is looking for someone who can express himself through movement beyond simply executing a combination technically.

Modern dance choreography ranges from the dramatic to pure motor action. Differing concepts of time, space, and energy are constantly emphasized in differing techniques; you should be prepared to handle improvisation in a variety of styles, not only for the audition, but as a valuable part of your training.

Sometimes the choreography for the company is done primarily by the director of the company; other times, it is a collaborative effort among the dancers (Pilobolus is a prime example). Some choreographers demand dramatic interpretation from the dancer in a specific role for a thematic work. One has only to look at the works of the late José Limón—*The Moor's Pavane* or *Missa Brevis*—to know why dramatic interpretation is all-important in his company. As a contrast to this approach, Alwin Nikolais developed a total-theater concept, which deemphasizes personality by use of props, costumes, sets, masks, special lighting, visual effects, and electronic music. Other choreographers and dancers, such as Alvin Ailey and Geoffrey Holder, have a creative approach that stems from traditional ethnic or folk forms.

The following interviews with Erick Hawkins, Murray Louis, Dan Wagoner, and Phyllis Lamhut establish the importance of "studying" with a specific choreographer as a means of auditioning. I feel that through this approach, a young dancer has the best opportunity to reveal his potential as an artist.

ERICK HAWKINS

Erick Hawkins remembers that not until his junior year at Harvard did he know that dance existed as an art form on stage. From that point on, it was a new vision for him. Through that vision, he has developed his own theory of a mature art that relates the artistic beauty of dance to other fine arts, such as sculpture, painting, and architecture, and especially the lively art of music.

> At the core of modern dance, I believe there is a change of consciousness in the way one thinks and feels in the body— dancing is like talking from inside. If you compare the aesthetic values of modern dance and classical ballet, we live

Michael Avedon

ERIC HAWKINS

in America where ideals are different from the Russian ideals of the 1890s. Because of this, the starting point has to be different. We have to *be* and *express* different things. American Indian and Eastern dance offer another aspect which differs sharply from the ballet form. The way you feel inwardly, psychologically, has a lot of variation in it. The Western attitude is: "Man's function is to dominate and conquer nature." I think that our starting point is that of cooperating with nature. If you feel that with your body, you are going to express it in your movement.

Modern dance has such a wonderful wealth of possibility, since the truth in the art form in general comes through change, so that the experiences do not wear out. Being able to have qualitative changes in training is important in achieving a happier life in this art form. Trendiness is the foolish trying to make innovations instead of making fresh statements about what human beings have always experienced. I once observed a young artist who did choreography that was not new in form, but original in its vision. Fashion can degrade an art form; inventiveness renews it.

I work to train dancers so that they are aware of general principles that can be used by *anyone*, because they are right with nature. Once you have these principles, you can specialize. All you can practice is theory. If you do not know what the theory is, there is no technique. These movement principles are essentially covert: training must start with understanding of kinesthetic support and correct placement of the body.

I spend a great deal of time focusing on the completeness of my dancers' training, analyzing the technique and quality of their accomplishment both in and out of classes and performances. Consistency of training is the only means of correcting one's image. When it comes to emotional content, I avoid violent movements because they are a waste of energy and an ignorance of efficiency. The movements should be models of the completeness of the soul.

[Most of Mr. Hawkins' colleagues consider ballet a major factor in the training of a modern dancer, but he believes there is a trap in that assumption.] If ballet is complete, you should stick to that form. If one's own theory of modern dance is complete enough, he does not need to go back to ballet technique. The total premise for the existence of modern instruction is that, if there is to be modern training, a new vocabulary and expression in that form must have a new starting point. Complete and correct technical training in modern dance will include all the virtuosity of ballet and will be even more inclusive because modern dance training, if it is adequate, is a definition and extension of ballet.

In order to intensify the art of modern dance, there must be the traditional relationship in which insights are transmitted from the teacher to the pupil. Students should have confidence in the teacher with whom they study, and liking him is a necessity. When a dancer is young, he cannot evaluate all the possibilities, so he must trust his teacher.

Sooner or later, the student should understand that he will have to do his own learning and can no longer rely totally on the teacher.

As for choosing a modern dance company, a performance observation by prospective auditionees is a valuable approach before making a commitment to the company's school or to an audition. The standard audition process amazes me. Given the technical idiosyncrasies of most companies, I do not see how a director can teach enough technique in an audition to gauge a dancer's suitability for that company. Only once, I held an advertised audition. From that audition, I accepted one dancer, who stayed with the company only for a short time, and rejected another, who later made the commitment to study with me and soon became a regular company member. Several of my dancers came to study with me after seeing the company perform.

Movement is not interchangeable. To perform a certain vocabulary, the dancer has to study that vocabulary. All dance vocabulary is based on some specific movement theory and aesthetic ideal. They have to come and study. They also have to know, deep in their heart, that aesthetically this is what they want. The best way to sense this is to see a performance. By that approach, they can see if the beauty and aesthetics are compatible with their inner and outer selves.

When looking into a [small] modern company, you must realize that there are very few financial benefits, but the job will be more artistically fulfilling than if you are in a big [ballet] company where you are moved around like a pawn. Is the dancer a tool or an artist? I hope that dancers take time to answer this question before making value judgments.

MURRAY LOUIS

Unlike the many years demanded for ballet, university and college dance programs play an important role in preparing dancers for a career in modern dance. Although students on the college level are usually starting dance rather late, it is feasible for them to achieve the necessary foundation and training to audition for a modern dance company.

Tom Caravaglia

MURRAY LOUIS

Murray Louis tours extensively with his company to university and college campuses and is able to observe prospective modern dancers. He often encourages those who interest him to study with him.

Every audition allows you to show the skill you have to offer the choreographer. If you have the opportunity to study at the choreographer's school, by all means do so. You will be that much ahead in the game. You should know the choreographer and his work before auditioning. He will want to see how quick you are in picking up material. The audition process can be a shock to a newcomer. The number of dancers at the audition, their skills, backgrounds, clothing, and the process of being herded around like animals are examples of what you are going to be faced with. You are totally on your own at an audition.

I suggest that a dancer who is serious about a dance career should enroll in a New York studio to understand the professional working process. Knowing "how to work" to prepare oneself for the audition is advisable. College discipline also helps you in that way. Remember an audition is an instant statement of your abilities and you must show this in the first three minutes. [Other hints that Murray Louis offers are:]

Do not get thrown by the audition. Keep your cool.

Realize that the auditioner is looking for skill, personality, projection, and physical appearance.

If you have these attributes, do not tighten up while auditioning. There is a considerable amount of tension that is held in the auditionees body; I have seen dancers pass out because of it. Have a reasonable breakfast; do not go into an audition hungry.

My major advice to dancers is not to be crushed if you do not get the position or job. There are many other auditions to attend, and life goes on. Do not get into that one-shot syndrome, meaning, "I must have this job or I will die." Discover that there are other opportunities.

Remember that the choreographer already has a fixed idea of the kind of dancer he needs, but there is always room for one who is "special" and "comes across" [projects well]. The audition approach usually depends on the choreographer.

Sometimes, there are cattle calls; at other times, auditions are intimate and sensitively handled.

My typical audition starts with an open call, from which I pick three or four people. I bring these dancers into class for observation, which is a kind of callback. Generally, these dancers can hold their own in class and live up to their audition potential.

In the audition, the dancers are paced through a small technical trial, which consists of skills that allow me to see elevation, extension, and torso flexibility. Then, approximately fifteen minutes is allotted for a company member to teach a movement phrase from the repertoire. I explain the quality of the phrase, so that the dancers understand what is wanted before they execute the movement. This segment of the audition gives me the opportunity to see the dancers' lyric and dynamic range and the quality they will convey in performance.

Those dancers chosen for callback are telephoned by the dance captain, but everyone, whether invited back or not, receives a call from the office. I never make a decision during the audition process. Although I frequently choose company members from the school, I do not guarantee company placement to the students. In the competition of an open audition, the successful dancer will be the one who shows great drive and conviction.

[During my discussion with Mr. Louis, the topic of agents for dancers arose. As with most of the artists I interviewed, he felt that only when a dancer reaches a certain status should he consider having an agent.] Dancers who achieve the status of being sought after, especially in the world of show business, should definitely find an agent. Many times, the agent will find you, if they know that you are a marketable product. [Having a business manager and an agent in one person is a combination which dancers should avoid. It is not only unnecessary, but dancers find it particularly unpleasant when their income is slashed by the percentage taken out by the agent and the still more substantial percentage taken out by the business manager. Standard agents and business manager's fees range from ten to twenty percent of income received.]

Jack Mitchell

DAN WAGONER

Dan Wagoner and Dancers consists of seven very talented artists. Five of those dancers were in rehearsal when I arrived at Mr. Wagoner's studio for an interview. I was graciously invited to observe the rehearsal, which had been scheduled mainly to help a new company member learn the repertoire. This gave me an excellent opportunity to view the working process between the company members and the new dancer, and to sense the wonderful unity among all the dancers.

When I first observed a performance of Dan Wagoner's company in the early 1970s, I was so enthralled with the free-flowing movements that I thought his choreography was primarily based on improvisation. I came to realize and appreciate through this rehearsal that the movements are set to specific counts and the division of movement phrases is rhythmically intricate. It also made me realize that the opportunity to observe the choreographer's approach through both performance and rehearsal is one of the most valuable means of exploring a company before auditioning.

My priorities in selecting dancers for the company are attractiveness, clean alignment, no unusual mannerisms, and intelligence. I also look for the ability to execute movement with accuracy, strength, phrasing, and dynamic change. Having a resume and portfolio is a form of courtesy, but the proof is the person within the audition situation. I look to see if the dancer can handle quality in movement and has the potential for training his instrument and the sensitivity and willingness to commit himself to my style of movement. I want the dancer to risk everything for the movement and to focus on achieving this end. It is never wise, however, to present a facade in the audition with which you are not comfortable, especially if you will be expected to maintain that image while working with a company.

You never know how two people [dancer and choreographer] are going to work, so I am constantly aware of other elements while auditioning. Even the diet or humor of a dancer leads to a point of view which I am always aware of in picking the people I want to work with in my company. Realizing that you are not auditioning for a nine-to-five job is imperative, but I demand total commitment from my dancers.

To avoid the frustration of unreasonable expectations from a modern dance career, a dancer should first find out what he wants in performing: the professional experience from a company he commits himself to, or the aesthetic choice of working with a specific company. The aesthetic choice is first, as far as I am concerned. If you are interested in working with a choreographer or company, make a statement in the form of a letter to the choreographer. Make it a formal, straightforward letter, informing him that you like his work and want to be a part of it. Working in the aesthetic realm is valuable, no matter if you are studying with the originator of a technique or an instructor from the original school. Be persistent in doing good work. Choreographing a work for yourself and keeping busy is beneficial in constantly nudging your career along.

Many modern pioneers found that doing commercial work provided them, in their early years, with the financial assistance to continue their interest in modern dance. Many well-known modern choreographers and dancers, such as Hanya Holm and Helen Tamaris, shifted back and forth from commercial dancing to modern dancing. One can set high standards in modern dance and still manage to do commercial work, but I believe that the most artistically rewarding work is not necessarily the most financially rewarding. Unfortunately, it is harder these days to move back and forth, since the concert work is so much more intense.

Young artists should also realize that, although it is a good experience for any dancer, New York is certainly not the only place for a dancer's career to be nurtured. There is a major lifestyle adjustment that one must be aware of before coming to New York. Organizing your lifestyle goes hand in hand with the organization of your career objectives: your emotional stability depends on it.

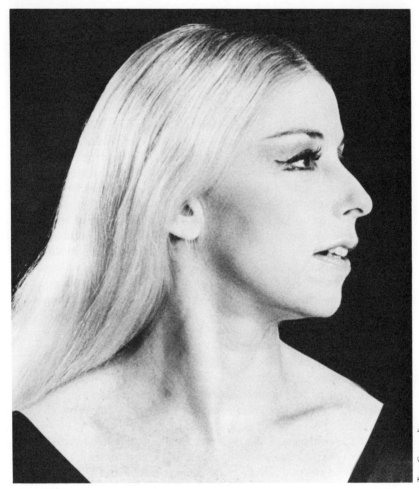

Tom Caravaglia

PHYLLIS LAMHUT

Phyllis Lamhut is realistic in dealing with those who are intent on making a career in modern dance. There are precise physical requirements, but good training and flexible approach are equally important. Having toured the United States and Europe, she has seen a great deal of growth in modern dance outside the major centers.

In order for modern dance to grow, one must continue to expose people all over the nation to this dance form. When students ask me about auditioning in New York, I say, "Why do you want to go to New York? You have so much going for you in this region. Why don't you start a company right here?"

For the training of a modern dancer, improvisation is important. The dancer should also respond quickly to correction. Sometimes, technique is not as relevant as the ability to respond and make changes. The technique I require for my work is not based on ballet technique. I emphasize a feel for expressing movement, rhythmic sense, and musicality.

The body should be released, so that the mind and body will work as one element. The body itself should be open, fluid, and strong—not regimental—with articulate motor skills, an open chest that is not blocked by tension, and legs that are free from the hip. Less technique and more artistry is a taste of fresh air. Awareness of dynamic range is crucial. Each person in my company is dynamic within his own body type. There are no lookalikes, the semblance of a company that is all the same, whereas the ballet corps in many companies has just the opposite requirements.

In auditions, the modern dancer should have good movement energy and a pleasant attitude. If you are an eye-catcher or have charisma, you may make it. Many modern dance auditions will deal with two major areas: improvisation and repertoire. I invite dancers from my classes to work with me, rather than having open auditions.

I believe that you have to be born to dance and love it to survive in this type of career. The physical work is only healthy if the attitude is good, and a good attitude is beneficial in helping one perfect and enrich his life.

7

DON'T CALL US, WE'LL CALL YOU—OR HOW TO FACE REJECTION

★★★★★★★★★★★★★★★★★★★★★★★★★★★★★★★★★★★★★

Rejection is not a topic that dancers like to think about in relation to auditioning, but they are often confronted with it. Unfortunately, there is no single solution for overcoming the disappointment of rejection, but there are considerations that may assist you in handling this often deflating situation.

You should remember that your talent may be only a part of what the auditioner is looking for in the audition. Height, attractiveness, body type, and personality are other factors that are often influential in the decisions made by an auditioner. Type casting and artistic decisions made by staff members other than the choreographer are other pressures over which the dancer has no control. If you are aware of certain requirements that may limit your chances at an audition, please do not feel that you should not attend. The more you audition, the more confidence you will gain in the long run. With a number of auditions under your belt, you will also achieve insights into particular qualifications that are required in your area of specialization. The luck of being in the right place at the right time could also be a factor in successfully finding employment.

With the threat of rejection in the mind of an auditionee, there is bound to be a certain amount of nervousness. Unfortunately, numerous talented dancers have fallen apart during an audition because of this. Even professional dancers who audition frequently are nervous each time they walk on stage or into the studio. It is only natural. Confidence is the prime element needed to stabilize your state of mind. Your training and accumulated experience in auditioning will help you achieve this end. Actually, I think it is healthy to be a little nervous; it causes the adrenalin to stir up your physical and mental alertness. The opposite is being so relaxed in an audition that vitality and sparkle in performance are lost. These extremes are what you have to guard against, especially if they prevent you from getting through the audition.

Settling some of your fears and lowering your level of nervousness might be achieved by analyzing this checklist.

Body Tension. Do you have problems with tension points in your body? If so, make sure you exercise those areas before auditioning. The neck, shoulders, and feet are a few areas where tension is held and are greatly affected by nervousness.

Organization. Did you bring your resume and required dancewear with you? If you know where everything is in your dance bag, you are more confident when you arrive at the audition. Prepare for emergencies: bring Band-Aids, sewing thread, a needle, and adhesive tape.

Mental Preparation. Have you psyched yourself up for the audition? If you have any misgivings about the audition, get rid of them immediately or come back another time.

Douglas Mackenzie

Rejection.

Physical Preparation.　Are you prepared physically for this type of an audition? It is imperative to keep up with your technique classes and watch your diet.

Type Casting.　Do you know what type is being asked for at the audition? Know the company's style, its artistic standing, and repertoire.

The Auditioner.　Do you know who is giving the audition and who the creative forces are in the company?

Drive.   Do you really want this job? Confidence grows when you know that you are going to perform the best you can for the auditioner.

In addition to answering these questions, you should review the list of guidelines given in Chapter One and the Helpful Hints provided by professional artists. Organization is a major prerequisite in achieving a successful approach. Dancers should reanalyze this approach for each job application.

I wish all aspiring young artists the same good fortune I experienced in my years of auditioning. I hope they continue to share, as did the interviewees in this book, in guiding future dance artists through the often misunderstood process of auditioning.

HELPFUL HINTS

★★★★★★★★★★★★★★★★★★★★★★★★★★★★★★★★★★★★★★★

APPEARANCE

Wear an up color! Do your best and bring a "sunshine" with you to the audition.

Geoffrey Holder

Have a clean appearance and do not wear anything that is not line-oriented. Do not get a case of the cutes when picking out your auditioning apparel.

Denny Shearer

Be careful not to wear excessive dance gear that is distracting. Shoes are important. If a dancer does not come with shoes, then he does not take an audition from me. The face is really important on Broadway, so do not have your hair covering it during the audition.

Tony Stevens

If you are called back for a show, by all means wear the same thing you wore the first day you auditioned. This will help the auditioners remember you.

Tommy Tune

If you are an extremely tall or short dancer in ballet, you must realize that you have to be just that much more talented than those in the average height category.

Richard Englund

For those auditioning for the first time, remember to smile and keep your facial expression alive no matter how aggravating the experience may be.

Murray Louis

RESUMES

Your resume should be simple enough to read that the director can scan it in five seconds. Less is better on the resume; do not stretch the truth.

Denny Shearer

Your headshot should look just like yourself in real life. A "composite," which is an 8" × 10" that shows several character shots of yourself, is helpful.

Tony Stevens

TRAINING

The best advice I can give young artists is this: if they run across someone they admire, they should attach themselves and feel the commitment to grow and learn from that person. Seek them out and stay close to them.

Lee Theodore

A dancer should be ready technically for the audition. Know what the audition is for and call or write in advance to see when auditions will be held. A letter of recommendation from a teacher that one has studied with is helpful, but not essential.

Robert Joffrey

A dancer should have the sense of being truly prepared, which comes with years of training. He should present himself as a

130

beautiful package: neat, clean, smooth, joyful, and with a vibrant presence.

Rebecca Wright

Ballet dancers should be fully prepared before coming to New York, and know which company they want to belong to artistically. One must admire the repertoire of that company and want to dance its ballets.

Robert Joffrey

EXPERIENCE

The truly talented performer can create a niche for himself despite the limitations of type casting.

Lee Theodore

If you want to get an interview with an agent or casting director, send him a picture and resume with a self-addressed postcard. On the back, type captions—Date, Time, and Place—for him to fill in the appointment information. I have had a good fifty-percent return on this approach.

Denny Shearer

If a choreographer gives you a correction, he is testing how well you pick up the correction and incorporate it.

Richard Englund

Formula: Technique; background of styles, other arts forms, and ballet companies; desire; drive; follow-through and consistency.

Rebecca Wright

I personally recommend that dancers telephone the director as a follow-up after mailing a letter and resume. Occasionally, I will allow a dancer to take a class audition, if he has taken the interest to contact me by telephone or comes recommended by one of the company members.

Donald Mahler

Loving what you see truly sustains the dancing career, so dancers should observe a company's performance before auditioning or committing themselves to a company's school.

Erick Hawkins

Patience is a real plus. With it, you will survive longer and gain greater pleasure from the whole process.

Laura Glenn

AUDITION BEHAVIOR

Always listen carefully to the choreographer during the audition and do not hassle him with a lot of questions just to be noticed. Technical questions should be given to the assistant choreographer, who is usually demonstrating the combinations.

Tony Stevens

Do not get involved with your competitors emotionally. Do not look behind you or you will lose your timing. Disciplined focus will also bring attention to yourself because you are so concentrated on what you are doing.

Lee Theodore

Of course, the second audition, or callback, is harder. They liked you before; now, give more of the same, but have a secret up your sleeve—a hint of another dimension.

Tommy Tune

If you want something badly enough, your ego should not get in the way. Rejection should never stop your determination to excel in your career objectives.

Charles Ward

Do not get thrown by the audition. Realize that the auditioner is looking for skill, personality, projection, and physical appearance. If you have these attributes, do not tighten up while auditioning. Show them.

Murray Louis

Be warmed up and ready to go.

Denny Shearer

Being courteous is a note to be taken not only when you are working with the choreographer and director, but with the stagehands and costume people as well. If you are not, it is very easy to get blackballed in future auditions.

Geoffrey Holder

Dancers alienate themselves when they try to categorize themselves. A true artist can do everything, so be open to whatever is given in the audition. Also, remember, being in front is not important—*being* is important.

Dennis Wayne

If a dancer can think of an audition as an extension of his work, it will be more beneficial to him in the long run. Think of it as a class and do it for yourself.

Dan Wagoner